LOVE AND PROPERTY IN THE
NOVELS OF DICKENS

Love and Property in the Novels of Dickens

By

ROSS H. DABNEY

1967
CHATTO & WINDUS
LONDON

Published by
Chatto & Windus Ltd
40 William IV Street
London W.C.2

★

Clarke, Irwin & Co. Ltd
Toronto

Printed in Great Britain by
T. & A. Constable Ltd
Edinburgh, 7

Contents

CHAPTER I

Early Novels

THERE is strong evidence in *The Pickwick Papers* that Dickens was, when he wrote it, already intensely interested in the relation between love and property. As one would expect, *Pickwick* is unique among Dickens's novels in the way it deals with attempts to make money out of love and marriage. In his other books such attempts are presented under the aspect of demoniacal villainy; they are involved with sinister and elaborate intrigues, forged and stolen wills, suppressed identities, frightened and withered children; in Pickwick mercenary marriage is the ambition of three relatively unthreatening and only moderately knavish characters – Jingle, Mrs Bardell, and Bob Sawyer. Dickens seems to be using heiress-hunting and a breach-of-promise suit as conventional sources of humour and of mild conflict and tension. But one notices with some surprise that the novel derives most of what continuity it has from Pickwick's relations to the schemes of Mrs Bardell and Jingle. Pickwick does not voyage at random; he flees Mrs Bardell and pursues Jingle. More exactly, he resists the efforts of Mrs Bardell to make money out of his alleged tampering with her affections, and he tries to protect women from Jingle's schemes to marry them for their money.

Mrs Bardell's lawsuit is the central action of *Pickwick*; again and again this lawsuit serves to hold the novel together. When Pickwick goes to Ipswich we know that he must come back to deal with Dodson and Fogg; when he goes back to Dingley Dell for Christmas we know that he must come back to stand trial, when he goes to Bath we know he must come back to prison as soon as Dodson and Fogg get a writ against him for the costs that he has refused to pay.

Pickwick's relation to Jingle's manœuvres is the same kind of connecting thread in the book as his relation to Mrs Bardell's. We meet Jingle at the beginning of the novel, rescuing the Pickwickians from the mob, telling tall tales in the Rochester coach, charming the rich widow Dr Slammer covets. He reappears at Dingley Dell, to steal Miss Rachel Wardle from Tupman. As Captain Fitz-Marshall, he is seen at Mrs Leo Hunter's party in Eatanswill; Pickwick pursues him to Bury St Edmunds and is tricked into the episode of the girls' boarding school (Pickwick believes Jingle is planning to elope with one of the girls). Later, Pickwick hears he is at Ipswich and goes there to ummask him and frustrate his attempt to marry an heiress. Finally Pickwick finds him, broken in the Fleet (where he also finds Mrs Bardell, similarly broken and ready to mend her ways). He relieves Jingle, and sees him shipped off to Demerara as a reformed character.

Pickwick's relationships with Jingle and Mrs Bardell have a good deal in common; besides determining events, and lasting through the whole book, they change in the same way; in both of them Pickwick is at first successfully cheated but finally enjoys complete triumph, heavily emphasized as the victory of his superior morality. Both Jingle and Mrs Bardell intend to make their fortunes by being bought off from marriage or compensated for the loss they suffer in not marrying. The bill of costs which Jingle makes out to Perker as his price for giving up Miss Wardle is paralleled by Mrs Bardell's damages. The two characters are, of course, in many ways complete opposites; Jingle is a highly sophisticated and remarkably sympathetic adventurer, quite conscious of what he is about, while Mrs Bardell is the first in a long series of Dickens's women who exploit their emotions and deceive themselves to their own advantage. It is notable that they should both be, in a sense, designing lovers. Dickens's hero takes shape as their adversary. As Pickwick ceases to take notes and collect objects, and develops from a spectator into a combatant, his preoccupations and activities become concentrated in one area; the fights in which he engages are all, in one way or another, against mercenary marriages or in favour of disinterested ones.

There are obvious advantages in this concentration. Dickens has his hero struggle in contexts peculiarly calculated to bring out a character of enthusiastic innocence and unworldliness. But mercenary marriage and designing pretence of love seem interesting to Dickens even aside from their use as convenient melodramatic devices of plot construction or objects to elicit Pickwick's indignation and demonstrate his character. Entanglement of money with marriage comes into the book through other people. Bob Sawyer feels that Ben Adams ought to have Arabella's thousand pounds. Winkle may be cast off by his father because these thousand pounds are not enough. Job Trotter supposedly has his eye on the cook, who will have a chandler's shop. One of the extraneous tales deals with a rich madman who buys a wife who despises him from 'her needy relatives' and drives her to madness and death (Chap. 11); another with little Nathaniel Pipkin, who dreams of 'softening old Lobbs, opening the strong box, and marrying Maria' (Chap. 17); and another with Tom Smart, who is anxious to marry the buxom widow and stand behind the bar of her comfortable pub, and who is enabled to do so by the discovery that his rival is a 'designing villain' (Chap. 14).

The comic perspective which governs the activities of Jingle and Mrs Bardell, of Bob Sawyer, Job Trotter, Pipkin, and Smart, sometimes keeps us from accepting the seriousness and importance of the values involved. It is difficult to keep in mind as one reads that Wardle and Pickwick really are, as Wardle says, saving Miss Wardle from a life of misery when they get her away from Jingle.*

On the whole, whatever ambiguity is involved in his comedy, it seems clear that Dickens means us to take seriously the villainy of heiress hunting and similar commercial exploitations of love. When Pickwick agrees to lurk in the garden of the girls' boarding school, he says he does not like the plan, but 'as the happiness of the young lady's whole life is at stake, I adopt it' (Chap. 16). The young lady is imaginary, Pickwick is to be made ridiculous, but this does not at all deny his values. Dickens takes Jingle's rascality seriously enough to be obliged to ruin him, humble him before Pickwick, reform him, and ship him off to the West Indies. This may

---

* This incongruity between matter and mood or tone is, of course, particularly important to the humour of *Pickwick Papers*; most of Sam Weller's cheerful similes and anecdotes are, in fact, extremely grim.

seem like a lapse of perspective as well as of taste; if so, it is because Dickens, becoming serious and sentimental, has forced upon us values which were formerly surrounded by the ambivalence of humour. Jingle's wickedness has lain essentially not in his insolence towards Pickwick (for which it would indeed be a lapse of taste to punish him) but in his mercenary trifling with the affections of ladies. Dickens has evidently kept this wickedness firmly in mind, even if he has (happily) made it difficult for his readers to do so.

The comic perspective on mercenary love found in *Pickwick* is rarely encountered in the novels which follow. Marrying for money, fortune hunting, the relation between love and property, become too serious and awful to laugh at. Except on rare occasions like Mr Bumble's appraisal of Mrs Corney's property, the perspective on these matters becomes melodramatic and explicitly moralistic.

In his second novel, *Oliver Twist*, Dickens uses for the first time a plot situation which he afterwards repeats, with variations, again and again. A child, Oliver, or Smike, or Esther Summerson, or Arthur Clennam, is deprived, through the medium of a mercenary marriage accepted by one of his parents, of the love and nurture which are his by right. Often the child is illegitimate and the mercenary marriage is seen as responsible for his illegitimacy. Usually but not always, the child survives this deprivation, and is strengthened or purified by his ordeal; sometimes he seals his survival by making a successful and disinterested marriage himself – in *Oliver Twist* this is done by proxy through Rose and Harry.

It is easy to overlook the role of mercenary marriage

in this novel. As in *Bleak House* and *Little Dorrit*, a calculated and loveless marriage is at the base of the mystery surrounding the protagonist's origins, which are explained late in the book; in *Oliver Twist* the mystery, the part of the plot which furnishes what one might call the external motivations of the characters (as opposed to immediate reactions motivated by no more than the reader knows) is difficult to keep straight in one's mind. Briefly, Oliver's father was forced to marry by 'family pride, and the most sordid and narrowest of all ambition. ...' (Chap. 49). The 'most unnatural issue' (Chap. 49) of that union was Monks. Later, separated from his wife, Oliver's father met Agnes Fleming and she conceived Oliver. During her pregnancy, the father had to go to Rome, where he sickened and died.* His wife and Monks descended on him as he was dying; she burned his will, which had bequeathed most of his property to Agnes and her expected child. Monks inherited his mother's hatred for Oliver and Agnes; when he found Oliver by chance he was willing to pay Fagin hundreds of pounds to drag him 'to the very gallows-foot', and to buy from Mrs Bumble the evidence of Oliver's identity. Mr Brownlow loved Oliver's father's sister, who died on what was to be their wedding day; this furnishes his motive for taking sufficient interest in Oliver's origins to pursue Monks to the West Indies to find them out. Rose is Agnes's sister, Oliver's aunt.

One can see that the original sin in the story, the violation which explains and justifies the guilty love of Oliver's

---

* The occasion of this trip to Rome is significant; it is to collect the money of a rich relative who had died there, and who is represented as one of those whose interest was served by the miserable marriage.

parents is the forced marriage, from motives of family interest, of his father. This forced marriage is thus the mainspring of the mechanism of Oliver's suppressed identity and stolen rights – the mechanism which sets him apart from other parish orphans and which at the same time subjects him to extraordinary persecutions and gives him the possibility of escape. It is a commonplace of the criticism of *Oliver Twist* that this melodramatic machinery, in so far as it matters at all, is a distraction from the real point and accomplishment of the book, a negation, or an attempt to draw the sting of what is really felt and said in it. But it is wrong to assume that the mechanism of conspiracy, forged wills, suppressed identity, etc., is uninteresting or unimportant to Dickens or that he made Oliver a little bourgeois as a matter of strategy in order to interest middle-class readers in the plight of parish children. Dickens is deeply involved, as in other novels, in the special, extraordinary position and rights of a particular child; the train of events by which that child's extraordinary position is explained is not to be brushed aside as without significance. Dickens shows how concerned he is with the opposition of mercenary and disinterested marriage not only by relating it to Oliver's plight, but by inserting the story of Harry Maylie and Rose Fleming, which has nothing directly to do with the main plot. Rose refuses Harry because he has powerful friends, ambitions and prospects, while she has no money and obscure origins:

'Yes, Harry, I owe it to myself, that I, a friendless, portionless girl, with a blight upon my name, should not give your friends reason to suspect that I had sordidly yielded to your first passion, and fastened myself, a clog, on all your hopes and projects. I owe it to you and yours, to prevent you from opposing, in the warmth of your generous nature, this great obstacle to your progress in the world.' (Chap. 35)

Removing the blight from her name makes no difference; her intent is firm. But Harry abandons his prospects, and drops his powerful friends:

'Such power and patronage, such relatives of influence and rank as smiled upon me then, look coldly now; but there are smiling fields and waving trees in England's richest county; and by one village church – mine, Rose, my own! – there stands a rustic dwelling which you can make me prouder of than all the hopes I have renounced, measured a thousandfold.' (Chap. 41)

The real association between this and the rest of the novel is a thematic one: the trouble started with a marriage made to satisfy family pride and ambition; the book ends with a marriage conceived as a deliberate rejection of these.

Dickens's next book, *Nicholas Nickleby*, more than any other of his novels, seems to depend upon conventional melodramatic attitudes, motives and gestures. As in *Oliver Twist*, the area of the novel which the plot specifically concerns is not particularly memorable. The book is usually remembered for Squeers and Dotheboys Hall; perhaps one also recalls the Mantalinis, Smike, Mrs Nickleby and her mad admirer, or the fat, benevolent Cheeryble brothers, pale shadows of Pickwick. But the skeleton of the book and a considerable portion of its flesh is made up of the plots of Ralph Nickleby against Nicholas, the outrages suffered by his sister, the position and origins of Smike, the plot to marry Madeline to

Gride, and the loves of Nicholas and Kate. In these, Dickens's concern with the relations between love, marriage, and money is strongly evident. He accepts conventional resolutions of conventional conflicts between love and money; he allows his hero and heroine to have the best of both worlds; he does not press to an issue some of the social comments and criticisms he seems constrained to make. In these respects – conventionality, inconsistency, relative timidity, Nicholas Nickleby makes a useful contrast to later novels.

To start with relatively unimportant matters, the persecutions which Kate must suffer from Sir Mulberry Hawk stem from their meeting in Ralph's house; Ralph has meant Kate as unconscious bait for Sir Mulberry's victim, Lord Frederick Verisopht, whose money Ralph means to have. Ralph shows some compunction about using Kate in this way, but justifies himself by reference to the way of the world:

'I wish,' thought Ralph, 'I had never done this. And yet it will keep this boy to me, while there is money to be made. Selling a girl – throwing her in the way of temptation, and insult, and coarse speech. Nearly two thousand pounds profit from him already, though. Pshaw! match-making mothers do the same thing every day.' (Chap. 26)

Kate is not in as much danger as Madeline Bray, who actually agrees to marry the ancient and hideous Gride in order that her father may be paid out of debt and pensioned. By gloating over Madeline's clustering hair, ripe and ruddy lips, little feet, etc., Gride tries to persuade Ralph that lust is his only motive for marriage. But Ralph knows better. In fact, Gride has in his possession a deed in Madeline's favour, and expects, as her husband, to collect 'some little property'.

Ralph, it turns out, himself married for money and, for money, concealed his marriage:

The same love of gain which led him to contract this marriage led to its being kept strictly private; for a clause in her [Ralph's wife's] father's will declared that, if she married without her brother's consent, the property, in which she had only some life interest while she remained single, should pass away altogether to another branch of the family. (Ch. 60)

The consequences of Ralph's greed in this instance include, eventually, his suicide. He has lived separated from his wife, hoping to keep the secret until her brother's death, His wife has tired of this and 'eloped with a younger man'; Brooker has stolen the child, Smike, and later put it in Squeers's school; Smike, as Nicholas's protégé, has become the object of his father's persecution. When Ralph finally learns that he has 'hunted down his own child to death', he hangs himself.

Nicholas and Kate, of course, eventually marry happily. Both their loved ones are richer than they; this inequality seems for a while, as it did to Ruth Fleming in *Oliver Twist*, an insuperable obstacle. When Mrs Nickleby tells Nicholas that Frank Cheeryble is in love with Kate, he quickly and sternly chastens his mother's enthusiasm. The family, he points out, is deeply in debt, in every way, to the brothers Cheeryble:

'What kind of return would that be which would be comprised in our permitting their nephew, their only relative, whom they regard as a son, and for whom it would be mere childhishness to

suppose they have not formed plans suitably adapted to the education he has had – in our permitting him to marry a portionless girl,
so closely connected with us, that the irresistible inference must
be that he was entrapped by a plot; that it was a deliberate scheme,
and a speculation amongst us three.' (Chap. 55)

Kate later declines Frank's proposal of marriage out of
the same sense of duty: ' "I told him," she said, in a
trembling voice, "all that I have since found you told
Mama; . . ." ' (Chap. 59). Nicholas, with respect to his
own affairs, is in the same position:

How base it would be of me to take advantage of the circumstances which placed her here, or of the slight service I was
happily able to render her, and to seek to engage her affections
when the result must be, if I succeeded, that the brothers would
be disappointed in the darling wish of establishing her as their own
child, and that I must seem to hope to build my fortunes on their
compassion for the young creature whom I had so meanly and
unworthily entrapped: turning her very gratitude and warmth of
heart to my own purpose and account, and trading in her misfortunes. (Chap. 61)

All this talk, of course, reduces simply to a question
first of money and second of what people will think.
Dickens allows his hero to seem willing to let his actions
be controlled by mistaken judgments and false values.
The presumption is that if one marries a person richer
than oneself the world will automatically assume a mercenary plot. Since what is right is not distinguished from
what is approved, matching one's partner's fortune
becomes a moral prerequisite to marriage. Nicholas is so
moved by Kate's fortitude that, we are told, if he had had
ten thousand pounds, he would have spent it all 'to

secure her happiness'; one realizes, with something of a shock, that this is no metaphor.

Here Dickens's position is a curious one. He is not being ironic, yet he is setting his hero to argue in favour of a family polity on marriage and against free choice and inclination: that is, against Dickens's own convictions. There is no argument or gesture like Harry Maylie's to show that Nicholas's values are wrong and harmful; rather these speeches seem intended to demonstrate his nobility and unselfishness. Naturally the Cheeryble brothers overcome all scruples and force the young people together: 'How dare you think, Frank, that we should have had you marry for money, when youth, beauty, and every amiable virtue and excellence were to be had for love'? (Chap. 63). One expects the Cheeryble brothers to do things like this, but one cannot take their virtue seriously; it is much less real than Ralph's villainy. Dickens manages to have things both ways: Nicholas is established as a noble and unselfish young man, yet he gets Madeline and her fortune. The point that beauty and excellence are worth more than money is made, but made, so to speak, by Andrew Carnegie, who not only can afford to make such points, but who also is not likely to impress anyone in making them. Even though Kate and Nicholas are penniless and their partners are rich, their loves and marriages are made to fit into a convention of suitability. Kate is no problem; it is always all right for a poor young lady to marry well once she has shown that she is delicate about doing so. Nicholas's case is complex. Madeline, his bride, has expectations from the rich Cheerybles not because of family ties, but because they once loved, respectively, her mother and her

aunt, and have always taken an interest in her.* Since
they have come to take an interest in Nicholas too, there
is, as he grows in their favour, an increasing equality
between him and Madeline in their relation to wealth.
The relative positions of Pip, Estella, and Miss Havisham are quite similar. Madeline also has her own fortune,
aside from the Cheerybles. But this fortune is discovered
and gained for her in the wild scramble at the end of the
book; it is not an established thing, and she would not
have got it without Nicholas and his friends (who were
originally not searching for the stolen deed – none of the
good people are really interested in money – but for
evidence to break the conspiracy to establish Snawley as
Smike's father). Nicholas is thus carefully protected by
circumstances from 'seeming to hope to build my fortunes' by his marriage, although he does in fact so build
them. One of Dickens's many didactic purposes in this
novel is to attack 'matchmaking mothers' (Chap. 26),
'good, rich, substantial men who would gladly give their
daughters' to rich old gnomes (Chap. 54) – the eagerness
of worldly people to better themselves by marriage. Mrs
Nickleby, in particular, is ridiculously eager, and
Nicholas is quite severe with her for it. But the priority
of the demands of conventional melodrama in *Nicholas
Nickleby* keeps Dickens from being consistent in this
matter.

When the scheme to marry Madeline to Gride has
been defeated by Mr Bray's death, and Ralph is trying

* It is interesting to note the similarity in this respect between the Cheeryble
brothers, Mr Brownlow, and the single gentleman in *The Old Curiosity Shop*. All of
them treasure the memory of dead loves astoundingly like, respectively, Madeline,
Oliver, and Nell. One is tempted to guess that this has something to do with the relation between Mary and Georgiana Hogarth in Dickens's mind.

to salvage some revenge out of the wreckage of his plans, he persuades Squeers to try to find the stolen deed in favour of Madeline, so that he can burn it;

> ... Ralph drew, with his utmost skill and power, a vivid picture of the defeat which Nicholas would sustain, should they succeed, in linking himself to a beggar, where he expected to wed an heiress. ... (Chap. 56)

In Dickens's next novel, *The Old Curiosity Shop*, the villain, also a usurer, gloats as he contemplates his revenge on Nell's brother and Dick Swiveller:

> 'After labouring for two or three years in their precious scheme, to find that they've got a beggar at last, and one of them tied for life. Ha! ha! ha! He shall marry Nell. He shall have her, and I'll be the first man, when the knot's tied hard and fast, to tell 'em what they've gained and what I've helped 'em to. Here will be a clearing of old scores, here will be a time to remind 'em what a capital friend I was, and how I helped 'em to the heiress. Ha! ha! ha!' (Chap. 21)

The difference in the issues of these projects of the two usurers is a measure of the difference in the structures of the two books, and specifically in their treatment of the relationship of love and money. Ralph is at the centre of the melodrama of *Nicholas Nickleby*, vitally concerned in all the plots and conspiracies; he is systematically and utterly defeated. In this instance Nicholas marries the girl, and she proves to be, after all, an heiress. Ralph's scheme is not as threatening as he thinks it is, since Nicholas does not expect to make his fortune by marriage. Still the threatened loss of the will is a danger to be reckoned with and defeated; the whole weight of the melodrama makes it necessary for Nicholas and Madeline to have her fortune.

On the other hand, Quilp, whose fantastic wickedness is far more vital and convincing than Ralph's, is curiously irrelevant to the plot of *The Old Curiosity Shop*; the only thing he does besides torment his wife and mother-in-law is to have Sampson Brass fix on Kit Nubbles a false suspicion of theft. Nell is not his victim, but her grandfather's. The plot to marry Dick to Nell is completely unreal; they never speak to each other and are only together once. While Nicholas, with the purest of intentions, makes his fortune by marriage, Dick, who means to marry for money, eventually first educates and then marries the penniless and nameless little servant girl whom he calls 'the Marchioness'. Dickens thus vindicates disinterested marriage far more genuinely than he did in *Nicholas Nickleby*, although this time the vindication is only on the periphery of the novel.

The relationship between Dick and the Marchioness is strikingly similar to that between Wrayburn and Lizzie in Dickens's last completed novel. There is a considerable social distance between the partners (Dick, who starts out making w's of v's, soon stops). The girl saves the man's life, he has her educated. The most important characteristic of these matches is one which they have in common with that between Arthur Clennam and Amy Dorrit: both partners are alone, they have spent most or all their lives without real friends, they desperately need each other's help. The idea of marriage as sorely needed mutual aid, as a private haven in a bleak and threatening world, is thus suggested in the match between Dick and the Marchioness, but not at all clearly or strongly; both he and she are too odd to be figures from whom one is likely to generalize or draw lessons.

Dick and the Marchioness have only a tenuous connection with the centre of the novel, the story of little Nell. This centre has, itself, to do with love and money. The sufferings of Nell and her grandfather are caused by the old man's desperate wish to make Nell rich. Nell urges what will become the lesson of later novels – *Bleak House*, *Little Dorrit*, *Great Expectations*, *Our Mutual Friend* – let us be poor and happy; the drive for unearned wealth only makes us miserable and wastes us away. Just as with Dick and the Marchioness, one is not likely to extract the moral. In *The Old Curiosity Shop* this drive for easy money is something remote, eccentric, depraved, obviously foolish, and doomed to failure; in the later novels it becomes more ordinary, more recognizably the obsession of a whole culture.

In *Barnaby Rudge* Dickens again constructs a plot around the issue of motives for marriage. There are three plots in the novel – one concerned with the Gordon Riots, one with the mystery of the murder of Emma Haredale's father, and one with the love of Emma and young Edward Chester and the quarrel between her uncle and his father. The three plots are brought together more or less mechanically – everything is involved in the riots. The Haredales are a Catholic family; Gashford, the mastermind behind the riots, has a grudge against Mr Haredale; Hugh, who is a leading spirit in the riots and symbolizes their fierce and desperate irresponsibility, turns out to be Sir John Chester's bastard son; Barnaby, whose father is the real murderer of Haredale's brother, is also a rioter. But Gashford and his master, Lord George Gordon, do not appear until Chapter 35, almost halfway through the book; up to this point nothing is said about the anti-Catholic agitation, and very little about the murder mystery. Most of the first half of the book is concerned with Sir John Chester's frustration of the love between Emma and Edward. The lovers themselves are pale and perfunctory characters – Emma is hardly seen and Edward is not much more than a foil to Sir John. This heartless, selfish, amoral man of the world, whom Dickens evidently intends as a hit at the standards of Lord Chesterfield's letters to his son, applies these standards in an area which the letters avoid. Sir John, unlike his model, is a poor man. Although ostentatiously indolent, he busies himself to separate the lovers, entering into a compact with his enemy Haredale (who cannot bear the idea of his daughter marrying a Chester), gaining control of John Willet, Mrs Varden and Hugh as instruments to stop the meetings of the lovers and to intercept their letters, tricking Emma into the idea that his son means to jilt her. His motive for all this activity is a simple one: ' "I couldn't afford a match of this description" ' (Chap. 12). He tells Haredale that he will explain this to his son:

I shall put it to him on every ground of moral and religious feeling. I shall represent to him that we cannot possibly afford it – that I have always looked forward to his marrying well, for a genteel provision for myself in the autumn of life – that there are a great many clamorous dogs to pay, whose claims are perfectly just and right, and who must be paid out of his wife's fortune. In short, that the very highest and most honourable feelings of our nature, with every consideration of filial duty and affection, and all that sort of thing, imperatively demand that he should run away with an heiress. (Chap. 12)

When he makes these points to Edward, Chester explains that he only expects his son to do what he did himself;

I was a younger son's younger son, and I married her. We each had our object, and gained it. She stepped at once into the politest and best circles, and I stepped into a fortune which I assure you was very necessary to my comfort – quite indispensable. (Chap. 15)

Edward has not been trained to make money; when he laments this, and pleads for the means to devote his talents to 'some worthy pursuit', protesting his desire to be allowed to 'try to make for myself an honourable path in life', his father calmly points out that the Chesters have nothing but credit and that there is no choice.

To make a definite end of his son's engagement, Chester goes to Emma and convinces her that Edward is planning to jilt her on the spurious grounds of being too poor to deserve her. Edward is no match for his father; the lovers misunderstand each other, and Emma breaks her engagement. Sir John's next step is to arrange for a mercenary marriage, but Edward refuses to cooperate, and is disinherited. He is not seen again until near the end of the novel, when he reappears to rescue Mr Haredale from the mob and Emma from the nameless fate intended for her by Gashford. Like Mr Jingle, Edward has been employed on an estate in the West Indies. He has 'got on well, and is prospering'. When Mr Haredale gives his daughter to him, it is with a state-

ment which establishes the propriety, in important
things, of the marriage:

In goods and fortune you are now nearly equal; I have been her
faithful steward, and to that remnant of a richer property which
my brother left her, I desire to add, in token of my love, a poor
pittance, scarcely worth the mention, for which I have no longer
any need. I am glad you go abroad. Let our ill-fated house remain
the ruin it is. When you return, after a few thriving years, you will
command a better, and a more fortunate one. We are friends?
(Chap. 79)

Haredale is 'a not inactive man among his sect', and intends to retire to a monastery; still, there appears to be
no difficulty about the difference of religion.

It seems clear that, although Dickens has tried to
establish Edward and his marital project as unconven-
tional and defiant of worldly standards ['and when
Edward's name was spoken, Society shook its head, and
laid its finger on its lip, and sighed, and looked very
grave'; . . . (Chap. 32)], the marriage itself fulfils these
standards. One has no doubt that the Chesters will
indeed 'return after a few thriving years' and settle down
to live upon their income.

There is something unsatisfactory about this, or
rather, about the relation it is supposed to have to Sir
John Chester's precept and example. Making money
fast in the West Indies seems the wrong road to the
consummation of an honourable but financially imprudent love and the wrong alternative to a false and
fashionable marriage – wrong not only because Jamaica
or Demerara are too remote and strange for us to see
Edward struggling there to earn his Emma, not only

because it seems too easy for him to refuse the easy money suggested by his father, and then reappear, arbitrarily enriched, to claim his wife. When Edward, in his first conference with his father, protested his repugnance against the plan that be become 'a mere fortune hunter', Mr Chester (not yet Sir John) attempted, with a little philosophy, to reconcile him:

'What in the devil's name, Ned, would you be!' returned the father. 'All men are fortune hunters, are they not? The law, the church, the court, the camp – see how they are all crowded with fortune hunters, jostling each other in the pursuit. The Stock exchange, the pulpit, the counting-house, the royal drawing-room, the Senate – what but fortune hunters are they filled with? A fortune hunter! Yes. You *are* one; and you would be nothing else, my dear Ned, if you were the greatest courtier, lawyer, legislator, prelate, or merchant, in existence. If you are squeamish and moral, Ned, console yourself with the reflection that at the worst your fortune hunting can make but one person miserable or unhappy. How many people do you suppose these other kinds of huntsmen crush in following their sport – hundreds at a step? Or thousands?' (Chap. 15)

No doubt Dickens intends this, like Chester's other opinions, as specious casuistry, no more than a self-serving attempt to justify idleness and wickedness. Yet it is interesting to apply the father's final question to the 'worthy pursuit' which his son does adopt. What sort of thing did occur on West Indian estates in 1780? How was the money made? How did this worthy pursuit and the society constructed around it differ from the slave-holding society Dickens violently denounced in *American Notes*, written the year after *Barnaby Rudge*? The answer seems to be that Dickens didn't think of these things, that the West Indies represents merely, for his purposes here, a remote place where gentlemen make money, in the tradition of *Roderick Random*.* What matters is the gesture of effort and self-help, and its opposition to the conscious, collected, elegant idleness of Sir John Chester. In this opposition Dickens is evidently at one with his new age, the age of Bounderby. To Sir John, money can be contaminated by the way it is earned ('I fear his father dealt in pork'); to Dickens, at this point, the origin of money is not enquired into as long as it is earned 'honestly' and by hard work.

What most specifically concerns us here is the way Dickens links the gestures and poses he detests – casual superiority, negligent aristocratic self-indulgence – as well as particular vices – sexual immorality, selfishness, cruelty, meanness with money – into a complex whose natural and characteristic expression seems to be a proclivity for marrying, or trying to make others marry, for money. Dickens has already represented something fairly close to this complex of vices and poses in *Nicholas Nickleby*, with Madeline Bray's father; a much later and more important parallel is Henry Gowan in *Little Dorrit*, one of Dickens's most interesting villains. Bray is a relatively simple piece of melodramatic machinery; Gowan is a complex character, consistently developed, integrated with high success into the plot of *Little Dorrit* and the structure of values it enforces. Sir John falls somewhere in between, as important to his novel as Gowan but not as carefully conceived. Sir John is a synthetic character, made up of two principles; in putting him together Dickens reveals inconsistencies and contra-

* This tradition is evidently quite alive in the 1840's – Cf. *Jane Eyre*.

dictions in his own values and ideas. On the one hand
Sir John is a caricature of a Chesterfieldian aristocrat,
clever, disdainful, mannered, coldly and discreetly sensual, careful of appearances, utterly selfish; on the other
hand he is mean and conniving, he plots for money, he
pursues deadly enmities. One part belongs to the specific
conception of the character; the other reflects a pattern
of traits which Dickens gives his villains in the early
novels. The essential principle of Sir John's wickedness
is cold hedonistic selfishness rather than pursuit of the
pure joys of acquisition and revenge. This principle,
which is what Dickens is essentially driving at in his
attack on Lord Chesterfield, is far more effectively enforced in Sir John's relationship with Hugh, and in the
history of indulgence, betrayal and indifference which
it evokes, than in his chicanery and petty meannesses.

But Dickens, lumping together the things he hates,
seems compelled to make Sir John into a kind of anti-
Pickwick; he points out how uninterested Sir John is, as
he rides along, in his surroundings, how careful he is to
avoid any sort of warmth or heartiness, how stingy he is
with those who serve him, piously blessing waiters and
chairmen whom he fees with the smallest possible amount.
Just as generosity is throughout Dickens's novels the
first of virtues, so meanness with money has to be the
concomitant of all vices. Sir John's small savings on
waiters and chairmen as well as his connivings against
Edward's happiness fit into a pattern which is preserved
in Dickens's work up to *Dombey and Son*. All the villains
in the first six novels, with the exception of the peculiarly
unreal Monks and the violent Sikes, are money-
grubbing, grasping, tight and mean. All of them except

Sikes make their livings by various forms of chicanery, legal and extra-legal; four of them are usurers. That Sir John should have so much in common with Dodson and Fogg, with Ralph, with Squeers, with Quilp, with Pecksniff (he is especially close to Pecksniff), is a startling observation. Dickens was evidently unable to think of serious villainy apart from the drive for money.

What is wrong with the combination of vices Dickens makes in his characterization of Sir John? The answer is, that although a man may be different sorts of villain, the vices Dickens particularly hates are in some ways incongruous. The greed of his early villains is something pure and spiritual – money is to be gloated over, not spent; it is enhanced not by what it will buy, but by the pleasure of gaining it in devious and cruel ways, and of saving it by little cheats and meannesses. The Brasses do not spend their money any more than Quilp, or Fagin, or Ralph Nickleby; they do not live any better by starving the Marchioness. Sir John, on the other hand, knows how to spend money for comfort and pleasure: 'As to the life I lead, I must lead it, Ned. I must have these little refinements around me' (Chap. 15). Sensuality and fastidious taste do not go well with avarice; elegant disdain and confident superiority do not go well with small plots for either money or revenge. Power in the state does not go well with pinching poverty, and in fact Dickens, although he had to make Sir John poor to motivate him, does not follow through on this – we find Sir John evidently thriving – knighted and made a member of Parliament – years after his son, by refusing to marry for money, has supposedly deprived the family of its last resource.

This incongruity of vices is partly concealed by the nature of Sir John's principal activities – frustrating honourable disinterested love and promoting mercenary marriage – which provide a kind of bridge between the coldly sensual aristocrat and the scheming hoarder of gold. Its appropriateness as a bridge may go a long way to explain the adoption of mercenary marriage as a kind of central figure of evil. Mercenary marriage, especially when forced upon unwilling partners, blurs distinctions, hides contradictions or, more kindly, submerges them in an inclusive image. It fulfils Dickens's requirements for an activity which can be at the same time conniving, acquisitive, tyrannical, selfish, and essentially ungenerous; which can be represented as the way of the world, institutional, part of the fabric of society; which presents images of cold commercial lust; which implies that reliance for a livelihood on social machination rather than honest work which Dickens pins on the upper classes.

It is a good idea, at this point, to examine more comprehensively the values and opinions Dickens reveals in his novels through *Barnaby Rudge*. Dickens, a young man who prizes warmth and generosity above all things, glorifies givers, spenders, hearty good livers – Pickwicks and Cheerybles. The antagonists of these good men are unscrupulous lawyers, mean cheats, conniving and usurious misers extracting their pound of flesh. So far, there seems a simple opposition between getters and givers; the former find their pleasure in pure acquisition, and in making people unhappy and getting the better of them, the latter in making people happy,

usually by showering money about. This picture is complicated both by Dickens's values and his intelligence.
First, Dickens has other prejudices besides those which
relate to generosity and meanness; he also hates abuse of
power (Nupkins, Bumble, Fang, etc.), snobbery (Mrs
Wititterly) and, of course, aristocratic arrogance and self-
indulgence. Second, Dickens is much too intelligent and
aware not to see inadequacy in the moral analysis of
society implied by the simple opposition of getters and
givers – for one thing, where did the givers get their
money? He is too perceptive to fail to understand that
the archetypes of evil suggested by this simple alignment – Ralph Nickleby, Gride, Quilp, Brass, Fagin –
are not particularly relevant to the real evils of society.
Putting it like this begs the question; one assumes that
Dickens was concerned to work out the real evils of his
society and to expose them. In *Pickwick Papers*, this is
not true, except in a small way. It obviously is true in
*Hard Times, Bleak House, Little Dorrit, Great Expecta-
tions*, and *Our Mutual Friend*. Clearly Dickens's determination to make a moral analysis of society grew along
with his confidence that he could do so and hold his
audience. We assume, then, Dickens's increasing concern to get at the springs of evil in his society and his
increasing unwillingness to settle for villains, no matter
how vital and fascinating, who are essentially small fish,
ugly eccentrics doomed in the nature of things to failure,
concomitants of an essentially satisfied view.

We find, in fact, that after *The Old Curiosity Shop*, the
important villains cease to be usurers, misers, unscrupulous lawyers, sinister hole-and-corner plotters; Dickens
keeps these characters in circulation – Gashford, Jonas

Chuzzlewit, Tigg, Vholes, Grandfather Smallweed, Uriah Heep, Blandois, Silas Wegg, etc. – but they are forced out of the centre by successful hypocrites with solid and respectable positions, like Sir John, Pecksniff, and Henry Gowan, by driven and obsessed mixtures of some good and much evil like Dombey and Mrs Clennam, by institutions like Chancery and the Circumlocution Office, by the fabric of society which arranges for young men to be rotted by their expectations.

While evil in society is less and less represented by sinister eccentrics, mercenary marriages, forced or spontaneous, attempted or achieved, not only continue but become more and more effective and important elements in their respective novels. A contrast between the use of mercenary marriage in *Oliver Twist*, *Nicholas Nickleby*, *The Old Curiosity Shop*, and *Barnaby Rudge* on the one hand and *Dombey and Son*, *Bleak House*, and *Hard Times*, to go no further, on the other, suggests that in the earlier group Dickens is thrusting in a theme with which he is obsessed but which he does not know how to use, while in the later group he is placing the same theme in contexts which it organizes and illuminates. This change reflects Dickens's growing seriousness about comprehensive social analysis, but most importantly, it shows his growing ability at planning and organizing plots. In *Oliver Twist* opposition between marriage for love and for worldly interest does not really serve the plot; it is more or less hung on to it in the stories of Oliver's origins, and of Harry and Rose. In *Nicholas Nickleby*, Dickens uses this opposition again and again, with Nicholas, with Kate, with Mr Bray, with Ralph, but one feels a conflict between its use as a convenience in writing melodrama and as a subject of concern in itself; the first use implies different values—values satisfied, for instance, by Nicholas's abnegatory gestures – from the second. In *The Old Curiosity Shop* the plot is not served by this opposition any more than in *Oliver Twist* – yet again it is brought in, again it is emphasized by an unworldly marriage appended to the novel. One of the plots with which Dickens attempts to give shape to *Barnaby Rudge* centres around a pair of worthy and penurious lovers struggling against their parents' opposition, but this plot is taken over by its villain and does not make the novel any more coherent.

What seemed to be, in *Pickwick*, a topic which with its familiar values and tensions could conveniently give order and continuity to an episodic book, becomes in the novels immediately after it an element of disorder. Of course a mercenary marriage like that projected between Madeline and Gride, with its conventionally established motives, conflicts, and urgencies, fits easily into the complex melodramatic plot. But it is important to notice that in his first five novels Dickens does not fit a mercenary marriage into a plot to the extent of allowing it to take place before his audience – all the mercenary marriages are either unrealized threats or accomplished facts in the background of the action, like Ralph's, Oliver's father's, Sir John's. And the pointedly disinterested marriages in which Dickens is clearly most interested are the ones which fit most awkwardly and arbitrarily into their plots, like that of Harry and Rose, or Dick and the Marchioness.

Up to this point this study has been largely concerned to demonstrate an obsession. In the books so far discussed, this obsession does not bear important fruit; that is, there is no clear relation between it and what is good, powerful, or memorable in these five novels. The same is true of Dickens's next novel, *Martin Chuzzlewit* – the first in which a mercenary marriage is actually allowed to take place – but not of the one after it, *Dombey and Son*. Both novels deal primarily with the relation between love and property, but this subject has much more to do with the quality and effectiveness of *Dombey and Son* than the theme of any of Dickens's novels has heretofore. The jump between the two novels thus becomes for our purposes a vital one, and the contrast between them illuminating.

CHAPTER II

Martin Chuzzlewit and *Dombey and Son*

Martin Chuzzlewit, published between January 1843 and July 1844, and *Dombey and Son*, which came out between October 1846 and April 1848, represent successive attempts at more unity and control. Probably because it is commonly known that the journey Young Martin makes to America was not part of Dickens's original plan, *Chuzzlewit* has the reputation of an extremely loose and unplanned novel.* *Dombey*, on the other hand, is widely considered Dickens's first reasonably unified book; as Kathleen Tillotson writes, 'it has unity not only of action, but of design and feeling'.† *Chuzzlewit* and *Dombey* were both conceived by Dickens as treatments of separate vices – *Dombey* 'was to do with Pride what its predecessor had done with Selfishness'.‡

Notwithstanding the reputation of *Chuzzlewit*, there is evidence that Dickens planned the book ahead and tried to stay with his plan.§ Forster tells us that 'the

---

* Forster writes that increasing the sale of *Chuzzlewit* was a less important reason for the decision to send Martin to America than Dickens's impulse to answer the critics of *American Notes*. See John Forster, *The Life of Charles Dickens*, II (Philadelphia, 1873), p. 64.

† Kathleen Tillotson, *Novels of the Eighteen-forties* (Oxford, 1954), p. 157.

‡ Forster, II, p. 337.

§ In his Preface to the first edition of *Martin Chuzzlewit* Dickens refers to the problem of organization: 'I have endeavored, in the progress of this Tale, to resist the temptation of the current Monthly Number, and to keep a steadier eye upon the general purpose and design. With this object in view, I have put a strong constraint upon myself from time to time, in many places; and I hope the story is the better for it now.

notion of taking Pecksniff as a type of character was really the origin of the book; the design being to show, more or less by every person introduced, the number and variety of humours and vices that have their root in selfishness'.* Pecksniff and his two daughters, Mercy and Charity, stand at the focus of the novel, involved in a main plot and two subplots. The main plot concerns Old Martin and his grandson. Pecksniff initially expects the two to be reconciled and hopes to ensnare Young Martin (and thus eventually his grandfather's money) with one of his daughters. Later, deceived by Old Martin's scheme, Pecksniff plans to have the money more quickly and directly, and means to cement his hold on the old man by forcing a marriage between himself and Mary Graham, Old Martin's attendant and surrogate daughter. The first subplot concerns Jonas Chuzzlewit, whom Pecksniff is pleased to secure as a rich (although exceptionally unpleasant) son-in-law, but whose marriage is not central to his story. The second subplot deals with the relation between Pecksniff and Tom Pinch.

In all three plots selfishness and unselfishness are primarily represented through the characters' attitudes towards love and money. Mark Tapley, aside from Tom the most purely unselfish man in the novel, long refuses to marry Mrs Lupin because, as her husband, he would step into an extremely affluent and comfortable situation; good John Westlock is eager to marry penniless Ruth Pinch; the basic decency of both Martins is indicated by Young Martin's ardent desire to marry a girl with no money and Old Martin's willingness for him to do so.

Dickens's organization of these three plots around a

* Forster, II, p. 45.

common theme, and around the figure of Pecksniff, is not successful. The most specific and immediate cause of this failure lies in the main plot, in the fatal effects of Old Martin's intrigue against Pecksniff. Old Martin's scheme is to convince Pecksniff that he is going to leave him his money. Thus persuaded, Pecksniff will eject Young Martin and hover about Old Martin until the moment comes for him to be disabused and confounded by a reconciliation between grandfather and grandson, when Young Martin, hopefully chastened and dutiful, will be rewarded with Mary, and their marriage will be suitably endowed. Old Martin's scheme is carried through according to plan, but provides no more than a mechanical (and largely irrelevant) frame for the book. The initial plot situation is, however, well designed to exploit the theme of selfishness more vitally and profoundly than, in the event, is done.

The main plot, centring on Old Martin, involves the relationships of four people – the two Martin Chuzzlewits, Mary, and Pecksniff. Old Martin intends his two dependants to marry each other, but he wants to play the role of the Cheeryble brothers with them, brushing aside the protestations of duty he anticipates from Young Martin and generously endowing his grandson's disinterested love. Young Martin's sudden announcement that he loves Mary and intends to marry her frustrates the staging of this scene, hurts his grandfather's feelings and drives him to assert his power. Young Martin, now defiantly and self-righteously one who is willing to sacrifice his prospects to disinterested love, goes straight to Pecksniff, whom he knows his grandfather despises, and establishes himself in his household. Up to this

37

point we have an intelligent variation on a conventional melodramatic situation (which is exactly that between the Cheeryble brothers, their nephew Frank, and Kate Nickleby). Whereas in *Nicholas Nickleby* everyone had the satisfaction of making noble gestures of abnegation and getting what he wanted anyhow, in *Martin Chuzzlewit* the young man's egotism and the old man's sense of power fall in each other's way and a quarrel develops which promises to be fruitful. This could have been the first instance in Dickens of the kind of accomplishment he achieves in *Great Expectations*: starting with conventional melodramatic situations and making them illuminate the assumptions and realities of his culture. Young Martin, like Pip, like Nathaniel Winkle, Edward Chester and a good many of the young men of eighteenth- and nineteenth-century novels, is dependent on expectations of an unearned income. Like Edward Chester and David Copperfield he determines to work his way to the possession of his lady. Old Martin, like the Cheerybles, like Miss Havisham and old John Harmon, has the power of riches, of patronage, of writing wills and changing them, of commanding expectations. This power is intensified and the situation is telescoped by his having authority over both young people. Mary is nominally his nurse and attendant, but actually her relation to him is daughterly. Her position is thus so acutely uncomfortable that it contains a strong potentiality for probing the sanctions of love and duty. The positions of the two Martins are well calculated for the kind of examination of moral decay wrought by social and economic circumstances which Dickens carries out in his later novels.

All these potentialities are missed; none of the three

characters in this central situation comes alive. Instead we have Old Martin's scheme, which chokes off any possible vitality or development in his character by making him sham senility and which drives Young Martin out of Pecksniff's house, and, in effect, out of the plot until the end of the book.*

Since Old Martin and his grandson are given nothing to do before their final dramatic reappearance, with more than two-thirds of the novel ahead there remain effectually in the main plot only Mary and Pecksniff. Pecksniff's connection with this plot is different from that of the other three; he is only an instrument in the relations of the others, but he represents a pure form of the selfishness which makes the trouble between the two Martins. Pecksniff is one of Chesterton's examples for the dictum that in Dickens 'the best figures are at their best when they have least to do'.† The only possible thing for Pecksniff to do in the main plot after he has dismissed Young Martin and before he is undeceived by Old Martin is to make love to Mary Graham, and he does it. His motives are mixed; he means to consolidate his control over Old Martin, but there is a startling element of greasy sexual aggression, an emphasis on his physical unattractiveness, on his 'flabby face', 'heavy eyelids', and the 'fat thumb' which 'traced the course of one delicate blue vein' (Chap. 30) in her imprisoned hand.

The immediate impetus for his approach to Mary is a

---

* Sending Martin to America does not wrench the plot out of shape. Since he has left Old Martin and been driven away from Pecksniff, and since the term of his exile and estrangement depends upon the working out of his grandfather's scheme, there is nothing for him to do until Old Martin arranges the dénouement except humble himself and cure his selfishness. This he can do in America just as well as in England.

† G. K. Chesterton, *Charles Dickens, A Critical Study* (New York, 1906), p. 149.

discussion with Old Martin in which the old man laments to Pecksniff that Mary has not been taught a trade and that there will be no provision for her after his death. Pecksniff presumably expects that Mary's economic position will drive her to accept him. Dickens manages to project in Pecksniff's intentions something close to a paradox – a match in which both partners are to marry for money. But Pecksniff has another weapon – the appeal to Mary's concern for the person she really loves, who will be ruined without her prospective husband's influence. (This device comes into its own in *Hard Times*).

Whatever Dickens hoped for from Pecksniff's assault on Mary, all that comes out of it is further evidence of Dickens's preoccupation with the idea of forcing marriages on unwilling people. There is no real threat or tension; we know that Old Martin is not really senile and will protect Mary. Whatever Pecksniff and Mary say or do to each other is deprived of importance – even of reality – by Old Martin's deception and manifest intentions. Becoming channelled into Old Martin's scheme, the plot ceases to make productive demands upon the four people centrally involved in it.

To set off against these losses we have whatever tension and excitement there may be in waiting for the unmaskings and reconciliations we know are coming; we have the big scene which will more than compensate Old Martin for the little scene his grandson's impetuosity cheated him out of. Clearly, by Old Martin's successful trap, and its culminating scene, Dickens loses far more than he gains. One can appreciate the lure of such a set-piece to him; one thinks of the awful scene between

Carker and Mrs Dombey at Dijon, or of Dickens's own journey from Genoa to London and back in November-December 1844 in order to read *The Chimes* to his assembled friends. But it seems obtuse of him not to have seen that the scheme which secured this set-piece would shatter the potentialities of his main plot.

Having set up a situation between the patron and the two dependants which asked for a kind of shading and discrimination, a tracing of relatively subtle moral dynamics among characters called upon to be introspective and to grow, perhaps Dickens found that he could not manage what he had created, and therefore liquidated his situation with the heavy dramatics of Old Martin's scheme. Certainly when Dickens tries to show gradual change in Young Martin's mixture of decency and selfishness he does it crudely and unsuccessfully – Martin is a kind of Nicholas Nickleby with streaks of Bentley Drummle. The amendment of his character takes place violently – he emerges purged from the swamps of Eden. Dickens avoids representing Old Martin's similar moral mixture and similar reform; he simply has the old man confess at the end that he was responsible for a good deal of evil and that he regrets many of his former doings.

The subplot centring around Jonas Chuzzlewit, with its complicated fraud and trickery, its violence and mystery, cruelty and guilt, is evidently a more successful vehicle for Dickens's talents at this stage of their development. Jonas has affinities with the usurers, plotters, and criminals of earlier novels – Ralph Nickleby, Squeers, Quilp, Sampson Brass, Bill Sikes – but Dickens gets more inside him, gives him origins and connects him

41

more explicitly to values and principles in society. He represents an extreme development of the operation of the acquisitive principle, but he is also convincingly sullen, cunning, frightened, belligerent, and desperate. Jonas's activities, which more than those of any other character bind the novel together, are diverse but consistent. He inherits, making inheritance an active rather than passive act of acquisition, he marries and, in doing so, collects another five thousand pounds, he is overreached by Tigg's appeal to his vanity and unscrupulousness, he is involved in the guilt of his past, seeks to free himself by desperate action, and in so doing is destroyed. Seen like this, his is a common and representative story, and a good one for developing a lesson on the operations of the principle of self in a commercial society. Jonas is linked to Mr Mould and Mrs Gamp through his father's death, to Pecksniff through his marriage, to the web of crooked finance and speculation which Dickens struck at in passing in *Nicholas Nickleby* and which he goes into more thoroughly in *Little Dorrit*. Finally Dickens thrusts Jonas into the complex of apprehension, murder, terror, the chase, and final annihilation which he has already presented in Sikes's last days, and which comes up repeatedly in later books.

The main plot, if Dickens had followed through with it, would have shown the effects of the power of money in corrupting the relationship between the generations. With Jonas and Anthony, we have a situation which at first appears parallel to that of the two Martins but which rapidly ceases to do so. Like Young Martin, Jonas is chafed by the authority – expressed in control over money – of the older generation. Both young men think

42

of marriage as a gesture of independence. But in the case of Jonas, who intends to kill his father, resentment and the urge to independence are embodied in their most brutal form. Old Anthony, unlike Old Martin, offers no resistance; he tries to help his son marry, and when he discovers the murder plot plans only to take a little money and move away to live quietly with Chuffey. He does not even change his will.*

As soon as Anthony is underground (suitably interred under the auspices of Mr Mould with no expense spared) Jonas travels to Wiltshire to pay court to Merry Pecksniff. The match between them is of high importance. Aside from that of the Bumbles, it is the first evil marriage actually to take place in a Dickens novel (this as distinguished from marriages like Oliver's father's which we are told about as part of the background of the plot). It is not, strictly speaking, mercenary; it is not forced in any literal sense, as Old Martin determines when he interrogates Merry (she says that if anyone tried to make her marry she wouldn't do it). Jonas's motive, one feels, is not primarily money; rather he is attracted and challenged by Merry's artful buxom kittenishness, and by her ostentatious disdain for him. He wants to catch her, and crush her (like Tennyson's Fairy Lilian), and he does. Dickens handles Merry's approach to marriage extremely well. She accepts Jonas out of sheer emptiness and frivolity — because her sister wants him, because it makes her momentarily important, because

---

* The title for his new book which Dickens sent Forster (13 November 1842) suggests that Old Martin is to change his will several times: 'The Life and Adventures of Martin Chuzzlewig, [sic] his family, friends and enemies. Comprising all his wills and his ways. With an historical record of what he did and what he didn't. The whole forming a complete key to the house of Chuzzlewig.' Forster, II, p. 44.

she likes tormenting Jonas and thinks she can keep this up after they are married. She does not consciously want a rich husband. But money and the corruption it works in decent values and relations are at the root of her marriage. Because Jonas is rich and Pecksniff values nothing but money he is eager to marry his daughter to a man who is obviously cruel, brutal, nasty, and the worst of companions. Because Merry has been brought up in a world of sham in which all social intercourse has been devoted to concealing the relentless workings of the principle of acquisition, she has no experience of truth, honour, or love, and no standard by which to judge Jonas. Because her role in the perpetual play by which Pecksniff makes his living is to be giddy and superficial she has no experience in thinking out the implications of her actions.

As opposed to the conventional melodramatic unrealities of *Oliver Twist* and *Nicholas Nickleby* this is really a forced marriage and a mercenary one; in making it vital and bringing it into the foregound of the novel Dickens has taken an important step in making effective use of his pre-occupation with bad marriages. But once Jonas takes his bride home, Dickens can no longer cope with the situation — he slides back into melodrama and cliché:

She went up to him, as it seemed, and spoke lovingly; saying that she would defer to him in everything, and would consult his wishes and obey him, and they might be very happy if he would be gentle with her. He answered with an imprecation, and —

Not with a blow? Yes. Stern truth against the base-souled villain, with a blow.

No angry cries, no loud reproaches. Even her weeping and her sobs were stifled by her clinging round him.

From this point the subplot constructed around Jonas becomes channelled into the relationship of blackmail and murder between Tigg and Jonas. Dickens is obviously fascinated by the awareness between murderer and murderee, the sense of power which the man has who has decided to kill, the intuition of his victim, the finality of the act, the bloodstained clothes, the terror of guilt, the sense that everyone knows; he makes Jonas a hundred times more sensitive and imaginative than he was when we first met him. As a desperate disguised figure lurking in a thicket with a club to bludgeon his blackmailer, Jonas ceases to be relevant to Dickens's theme of selfishness; this sort of thing is different from putting poison in one's father's cough medicine in order to inherit. Patricide, grotesque as it is, has a specific connection with Jonas's background and education and with Dickens's theme; murdering a blackmailer because there seems to be no other way to escape the fear he embodies has no such specific relevance: it is an act in which the reader is expected to involve himself. Thus the Jonas subplot goes off on a tangent and ceases to be a unifying agent in the book.

The main plot loses its direction in the mechanics of Old Martin's scheme; the subplot, made of cruder and more grotesque materials, abandons its unifying function when it becomes involved in what may be called the Bill Sikes syndrome. There remains Tom Pinch's story, much smaller than the other plots but essentially separate from them and clearly of great importance. Tom is the incarnation of unselfishness. He has no sense of his own value or claims. He worships his employer, and is the only character in the book who, brought in contact with Pecksniff for any length of time, fails to see through him. Tom's function is to be put upon. In him goodness and lack of self-will are pushed to a point where they become stupidity; Tom's helplessness is an invitation for evil to fatten on him. Dickens makes a point of how wrong it is for Young Martin to patronize him, but cannot help patronizing him himself.

Like Smike in *Nicholas Nickleby*, Tom conceals a hopeless love for someone intended for a more conventional hero. Tom is in love with Mary Graham, but his loyalty to Young Martin, as well as his sense of his own unworthiness, keeps him silent. There are other Dickens characters in Tom's situation or not far from it. Toots, John Jarndyce, Young John Chivery, Sidney Carton, even Arthur Clennam and Joe Gargery, although these last two, like Tom too meek and withdrawing to be conventional heroes, are allowed to marry their loved ones in the end. The figure of the good man who magnanimously steps aside occurs repeatedly in Dickens. Sometimes he is a Smike, or a Toots, and has no real claims to press; sometimes he is a John Jarndyce, and gives up something he could have had. In his early comic form (Dick Swiveller and Toots) he is rewarded with a comic heroine of a lower class; in his latest form, as Joe Gargery, he takes the real heroine away from the protagonist. In his most famous incarnation – Sidney Carton – he makes a dramatic sacrifice, but his more characteristic position at the end of the story is one of placid abnegation.

The man who steps aside always has some disability which prevents him from properly aspiring to the possession of the heroine. Smike has been battered and starved

46

into near-idiocy, Toots has been fatally conditioned by Dr Blimber's academy, Carton has been dissolute, Jarndyce is too old, Clennam thinks he is too old. Only once – in Dickens's 1857 Christmas story, 'The Perils of Certain English Prisoners' – is the disability unequivocally a matter of class, and in this instance the gulf is extremely wide (the young man is an illiterate trooper in love with an officer's daughter). Tom Pinch's disability is partly his class – Tom's mother was a housekeeper and he is a kind of servant himself – and partly physical – he is 'extremely short-sighted and prematurely bald'; he has 'a great stoop in his shoulders' (Chap. 2). But we come to have the sense that what really keeps Tom from being a serious contender for life's prizes is modesty and humility – a kind of ultimate selflessness. Morally he is much finer than Young Martin.

There is a potential paradox in the by-play of two assumptions particularly strong in Dickens's time: on the one hand that the greatest moral excellence should be rewarded with the heroine's love; on the other hand that more moral excellence belongs to the man who steps back in humility than to the man who presses forward to take the prize. There are obvious ways to avoid this paradox or to play it down; one can, for instance, make marrying the heroine a more generous action by disfiguring her or taking all her money away. Or one can do away with egotism and competition by giving the unsuccessful contenders really fatal disabilities, like Smike's idiocy (this at the cost of reducing the weight and importance of their humility).

But Dickens lessens the reality of Tom's defects as the novel goes on, and emphasizes his fineness more and more. At the same time he insists on the intensity of Tom's love, the anguish it causes him and his determination never to reveal it. The imaginative reader begins to wish that Mary would conquer his scruples and take him. This is an effect that Dickens does not achieve with Smike or Toots. Inspiring his readers to a wish patently incapable of realization makes that reader query the conditions which make his wish unrealizable; the situation of Tom Pinch at the end of *Martin Chuzzlewit* inspires one to think more than one otherwise might about the marriage which closes up the book.

This marriage is unreal and thoroughly unsatisfactory. Of course Mary and Martin have not been made real to us as people who physically desire each other; this is to be expected. But they are just as blank as social beings – we cannot imagine what they would say or do in a quiet evening together (as we could, say, with Dick Swiveller and the Marchioness). One might expect the marriage to compensate for unreality by moral appropriateness. The book is about selfishness. Tom Pinch is unselfish, nowhere more so than in the suppression of his love. Martin is selfish, nowhere more so than in his disregard of the suffering which Mary undergoes through his love for her. Having made a sudden reformation in a context remote from Tom and Mary, Martin gets the girl. Tom deserves her more, and for all we are shown, seems to need her more. But this brings us back to the paradox, which, of course, only becomes obtrusive when one looks at a marriage in terms of its moral appropriateness. What makes Tom deserve Mary more and need her more is the same thing which keeps him from getting her. Martin's marriage is not morally appropriate; by pounding away at the sufferings of Tom Pinch Dickens makes us realize this.

But marriage itself, by its very nature, is apt not to be appropriate according to a morality organized around unselfishness, humility, generosity, and disinterestedness. Quite aside from whatever extraneous motives – of money or position – there may be, marrying necessarily involves a man's willingness to impose himself permanently, with all his defects, upon another person's life. This is intrinsically immodest, especially in a culture which theoretically exalts women, and yet believes in male authority in marriage.

After *Martin Chuzzlewit* Dickens takes pains (except in one book, *David Copperfield*) to neutralize this immodesty in every marriage he permits a hero to make. Florence Dombey is homeless and fleeing; to take her is to rescue her. Esther's beauty has been ruined; Amy Dorrit has lost all her money; Bella is raised from poverty by her marriage; Lizzie Hexam is lifted several rungs up the class ladder. In *Martin Chuzzlewit* the emphasis on Tom Pinch may be taken to indicate the strength of Dickens's awareness of the moral inappropriateness of Young Martin's marriage to Mary. Significantly, the novel ends (just after Augustus Moddle's escape from forced marriage) not with a vista of Young Martin's domestic happiness, but with a glimpse of the relationship in years to come between Tom and his sister Ruth:

And coming from a garden, Tom, bestrewn with flowers by children's hands, thy sister, little Ruth, as light of foot and heart as in the old days, sits down beside thee. From the Present and the Past, with which she is tenderly entwined in all thy thoughts, thy strain soars onward to the Future. As it resounds, within thee and without, the noble music, rolling round ye both, shuts out the grosser prospects of an earthly parting, and uplifts ye both to Heaven! (Chap. 54)

With the Tom Pinch subplot, then, Dickens suggests an insight into the relations between will, selfishness, and success in love; as with the main plot concerning the two Martins he does not follow through – he does no more than pick at the problem. *Martin Chuzzlewit* is a disorganized novel, but it is not a random collection of characters and incidents haphazardly put together. The structures through which Dickens attempts to organize it fail almost entirely; they are too ambitious – they demand a complex and subtle working out of relationships, an ability to withstand the lure of obvious dramatic effects which Dickens does not yet have.

Dombey and Son is more successfully organized. In this novel, as John Butt and Kathleen Tillotson show, Dickens was working carefully to reconcile serial publication with the development of a set theme in a complicated plot, making a plan for each number before he started on it.* There was also an overall plan; the most complete and detailed extant description of it occurs in Dickens's letter to Forster of 25 July 1846, which he sent with the manuscript of the first four chapters. This letter survives only in extracts printed in Forster's biography; I quote as much of it as concerns *Dombey and Son*:

* John Butt and Kathleen Tillotson, *Dickens at Work* (London, 1957), pp. 90-113.

I will now go on to give you an outline of my immediate intentions in reference to Dombey. I design to show Mr D. with that one idea of the Son taking firmer and firmer possession of him, and swelling and bloating his pride to a prodigious extent. As the boy begins to grow up, I shall show him quite impatient for his getting on, and urging his masters to set him great tasks, and the like. But the natural affection of the boy will turn towards the despised sister; and I purpose showing her learning all sorts of things, of her own application and determination, to assist him in his lessons; and helping him always. When the boy is about ten years old (in the fourth number), he will be taken ill, and will die; and when he is ill, and when he is dying, I mean to make him turn always for refuge to the sister still, and keep the stern affection of the father at a distance. So Mr Dombey – for all his greatness, and for all his devotion to the child – will find himself at arms' length from him even then; and will see that his love and confidence are all bestowed upon his sister, whom Mr Dombey has used – and so has the boy himself, too, for that matter – as a mere convenience and handle to him. The death of the boy is a death-blow, of course, to all the father's schemes and cherished hopes; and 'Dombey and Son', as Miss Tox will say at the end of the number, 'is a Daughter after all'. . . . From that time I purpose changing his feelings of indifference and uneasiness towards his daughter into a positive hatred. For he will always remember how the boy had whispered to her, and would take things only from her hand, and never thought of him. . . . At the same time I shall change *her* feeling towards *him* for one of a greater desire to love him, and to be loved by him; engendered in her compassion for his loss, and her love for the dead boy whom, in his way, he loved so well too. So I mean to carry the story on, through all the branches and offshoots and meanderings that come up; and through the decay and downfall of the house, and the bankruptcy of Dombey, and all the rest of it; when his only staff and treasure, and his unknown Good Genius always, will be this rejected daughter, who will come out better than any son at last, and whose love for him, when discovered and understood, will be his bitterest reproach. For the struggle with himself which goes on in all such obstinate natures, will have ended then; and the sense of his injustice, which you may be sure has never quitted him, will have at last a gentler office than that of only making him more harshly unjust. . . . I rely very much on Susan Nipper grown up, and acting partly as Florence's maid, and partly as a kind of companion to her, for a strong character throughout the book. I also rely on the Toodles, and on Polly, who, like everybody else, will be found by Mr Dombey to have gone over to his daughter and become attached to her. This is what cooks call 'the stock of the soup'. All kinds of things will be added to it, of course. . . . About the boy, who appears in the last chapter of the first number, I think it would be a good thing to disappoint all the expectations that chapter seems to raise of his happy connection with the story and the heroine, and to show him gradually and naturally trailing away, from that love of adventure and boyish lightheartedness, into negligence, idleness, dissipation, dishonesty, and ruin. To show, in short, that common, everyday, miserable declension of which we know so much in our ordinary life; to exhibit something of the philosophy of it, in great temptations and an easy nature; and to show how the good turns into bad, by degrees. If I kept some little notion of Florence always at the bottom of it, I think it might be made very powerful and very useful. What do you think? Do you think it may be done, without making people angry? I could bring out Solomon Gills and Captain Cuttle well, through such a history; and I decry, anyway, an opportunity for good scenes between Captain Cuttle and Miss Tox. This question of the boy is very important. . . . Let me hear all you think about it. Hear! I wish I could.*

Dickens's main plot – his 'stock of the soup' has similarities to the main plot he projected for *Martin Chuzzlewit*: both concern the relation between the generations

* Forster, II, pp. 339-41.

and the effect of pride on love. The letter to Forster emphasizes the gradual changes which are to take place in the father's feelings, the growing momentum of injustice, suspicion, and harshness, the tension within Dombey, and how it is to lead to his reformation. All this is the kind of thing the main plot of *Martin Chuzzlewit* demanded and was not provided with.

The two most important differences between the two plots are that Florence, unlike Young Martin, is to be constant, steady, always yearning and loving – to provide no reasonable ground for estrangement and suspicion, and that Dombey, unlike Old Martin, is to be stripped of his power – to fall into bankruptcy. The first difference is a disadvantage to *Dombey and Son*: Florence's character and role are necessarily extremely simple and it is hard to do much with her without monotony. The second difference is vital, and represents an important step in the evolution of Dickens's plots. He finally escapes from reliance on the good rich man who puts everything right in the end by showering guineas; without abandoning this convenient figure Dickens could not deal radically and seriously with the social themes of his middle and late novels.*

Dickens's plan provides for all important events through the death of Paul (which, however, takes place in the fifth, not the fourth number). After that, with three-quarters of the story still to come, it sets out definitely only the changing attitudes between Dombey

---

* Boffin, in *Our Mutual Friend*, represents a return to this figure, but with important differences, chief among which are his comic illiteracy, his extravagant play-acting, and the wild contrast he and Mrs Boffin make to the upper-middle class 'Society' of the book.

and Florence, the decay and downfall of the firm, and the decline into dishonesty and ruin of Walter Gay. Of these, only the relationship of Dombey and daughter is carried out as planned. Walter Gay (presumably due to Forster's advice)* is allowed to be a conventional (although largely absent) hero, and the decline of Dombey and Son into bankruptcy is huddled in at the close of the book. We are told of the danger to the firm in Chapter 53; we are told of its fall in one sentence at the beginning of Chapter 58. Butt and Tillotson conclude that a much more detailed treatment was intended, and that Dickens was distracted by Dombey's domestic affairs:

> ... for nearly three years, and three-quarters of the novel, Mr Dombey has neglected Dombey and Son, and Dickens has let private life overrun his 'business' novel. The situation has its own irony, but the cover and the letter to Forster are evidence that it was not what was originally intended.†

The difficulties in regarding *Dombey and Son* as a 'business' novel on the basis of its title, pictures of cash boxes and ledgers on the covers and a plan which, after all, stresses the relation between the businessman and his daughter, should not obscure the accurate observation behind this comment. Dombey's private life – specifically, his second marriage – has evidently wrenched the novel into a shape which was not planned. The marriage between Dombey and Edith, which takes place exactly halfway through the book, comes to dominate it. This marriage is Dombey's nemesis and accomplishes his fall; it destroys the villain Carker, it drives Florence out

* Forster, II, p. 341.   † Butt and Tillotson, p. 109.

of the Dombey house and makes possible her marriage to Walter. More emphatically than Dombey's relation with his daughter, it dramatizes the folly of allowing one's approach to the people around one to be controlled by the consciousness of one's wealth and grandeur. Yet it is not mentioned in the letter to Forster; the only possible reference to it as part of Dickens's plan for the book is the tiny picture in the top right-hand corner of the number covers of a stiff-necked man being married by a fat priest. It is hard to escape the conclusion that Dickens has allowed his novel – not so much a 'business' novel as a book about a proud rich man who refuses, like Scrooge, to respond to human requirements of love and kindness – to be taken over by another mercenary marriage.

The marriage gives no impression, however, of being forced into the story. It is in all circumstantial aspects extremely appropriate. Edith is a widow, Dombey a widower; he is rich, she has aristocratic connections. Dombey needs a son to carry on the firm and to reflect his own greatness; since Paul is dead, another must be brought into being. Dombey has ascertained that Edith is fertile; she has had a son by her former husband. Unlike the former Mrs Dombey, Edith seems strong and haughty, obviously capable of 'making an effort'. As a calculated and arranged marriage this one is thus a kind of classic. It is invested with the heaviest ironies, the most obvious significances, the fullest elaborations of any mercenary marriage in Dickens. We go through the wedding service and listen to the nuptial pair make their responses. Major Bagstock, Cousin Feenix, Mrs Skewton, and Mr Carker are present. Carker, who has already been related to the marriage with a good deal of sinister significance, kisses the bride and 'wishes her all happiness':

'If wishes,' says he in a low voice, 'are not superfluous, applied to such a union.'
'I thank you, sir,' she answers, with a curled lip, and a heaving bosom. (Chap. 31)

By this time the curled lip is wearisomely familiar. Edith is presented to us in a series of set scenes – with her mother, with Dombey, with Florence, with Carker. Her role in each relation is stereotyped and predictable. With her mother she is scornful; with Carker, whom she instinctively hates, she is disgusted, guilty and ashamed; with Florence she is gentle and motherly; with Dombey she is impassive except on the occasion when she makes her appeal. Dickens's concept of her character rests heavily on the idea of conscious self-degradation. Marrying Dombey is implicitly equated with prostitution; Dickens labours the parallel with the other mother and daughter, Good Mrs Brown and Alice Marwood (Alice is a prostitute, brought low in the first place by Carker). Dickens intended Edith to become Carker's mistress and to die; he evidently softened this partly because of Jeffrey's intuitions and partly because of his own relish for grand scenes.*

Both Edith and Alice, however degraded, are somehow not to blame: it is their mother's fault. Mrs Skewton and

---

* 'Note from Jeffrey this morning who won't believe (positively refuses) that Edith is Carker's mistress. What do you think of a kind of inverted Maid's Tragedy and a tremendous scene of her undeceiving Carker and giving him to know that she never meant that?' Forster, II, p. 364.

Mrs Brown, lacking their daughters' moral sensitivity, have led Edith and Alice into guilt and shame which they themselves are incapable of feeling. Edith's marriage is forced on her; she only accepted it because she thought it less humiliating to be sold than to be for sale. In her big scene with Dombey she reminds him that she made no effort to please him or catch him, that she never pretended to love him, that she always made plain her understanding that she was only an object with certain attributes and capabilities to be bought. Somehow this is supposed to mitigate her responsibility – this, and the terrible condemnation she is willing to bring upon herself as an adulteress. Dickens seems to go along with a convention which blurs women's real responsibility for their actions by exhibiting their anguished sensibilities and the cruel and arbitrary punishments they accept.

The moral difference between Dombey and Edith is that Dombey sees nothing wrong with making their marriage a bargain, an essentially commercial relation, while she knows they have done wrong, and feels cheap, guilty, and desperate in the relationship. This is the difference which makes Dombey's side of the marriage, critically considered, a success, and hers a failure. That Dombey should act the way he does with his wife is appropriate, and drives home the implications of Dombeyism. That she should combine so much will, passion, pride and analytical understanding of her position with a willingness to enter it in the first place has a falseness about it however plausibly it may be explained, and has much to do with turning her into a vehicle of interesting tensions, an engine of melodrama. In *Bleak House* and *Hard Times* Dickens succeeds much better with parallel characters and situations by avoiding this kind of strain on probability and the melodramatic intensity which goes with it. Lady Dedlock presumably has married for position not love, but her husband loves her and treats her with fine consideration. Louisa Gradgrind marries the horrible Bounderby not as part of a bargain for money or position, but to serve her brother.

Up to *Dombey and Son* there has always been a split between Dickens's two approaches to the mercenary marriages in his books – two ways of looking at them, crudely describable as melodramatic and social-analytical. In his melodramatic mode Dickens is working for conventional responses to conventional stimuli; in his social-analytic mode he is thinking originally about characters and situations he has conceived and, to some extent, about his society. The melodramatic is overwhelmingly preponderant in *Nicholas Nickleby*, not so preponderant in Jonas's marriage to Merry Chuzzlewit.

With the mercenary marriage which comes to dominate *Dombey and Son*, Dickens is able at the same time to indulge his melodramatic proclivities and to achieve a new level of serious social and psychological analysis. The resulting mixture is evident not only in the large perspective of courtship, marriage, battle, flight, pursuit, Carker's destruction, Dombey's despair, but also in the very texture of dialogue and description. Here is an illustration; Edith has just proposed to her husband that they both 'forbear':

'We are a most unhappy pair, in whom, from different causes, every sentiment that blesses marriage or justifies it is rooted out; but in the course of time, some friendship, or some fitness for each other, may arise between us. I will try to hope so, if you will make the endeavour too; and I will look forward to a better and a happier use of age than I have made of youth or prime.'

Throughout she had spoken in a low, plain voice, that neither rose nor fell; ceasing, she dropped the hand with which she had enforced herself to be so passionless and distinct, but not the eyes with which she had so steadily observed him.

'Madam,' said Mr Dombey, with his utmost dignity, 'I cannot entertain any proposal of this extraordinary nature.'

She looked at him yet, without the least change. 'I cannot,' said Mr Dombey, rising as he spoke, 'consent to temporise or treat with you, Mrs Dombey, upon a subject as to which you are in possession of my opinions and expectations. I have stated my *ultimatum*, madam, and have only to request your very serious attention to it.'

To see the face change to its old expression, deepened in intensity! To see the eyes droop as from some mean and odious object! To see the lighting of the haughty brow! To see scorn, anger, indignation, and abhorrence starting into light, and the pale blank earnestness vanish like a mist! He could not choose but look, although he looked to his dismay.

'Go, sir!' she said, pointing with an imperious hand towards the door. 'Our first and last confidence is at an end. Nothing can make us stranger to each other than we are henceforth.'

'I shall take my rightful course, madam,' said Mr Dombey, 'undeterred, you may be sure, by any general declamation.'

She turned her back upon him, and, without reply, sat down before her glass.

'I place my reliance on your improved sense of duty, and more correct feeling, and better reflection, madam,' said Mr Dombey.

She answered not one word. He saw no more expression of any heed of him, in the mirror, than if he had been an unseen spider on the wall, or beetle on the floor, or, rather, than if he had been the one or other, seen and crushed when she last turned from him, and forgotten among the ignominious and dead vermin of the ground.

He looked back, as he went out at the door, upon the well-lighted and luxurious room, the beautiful and glittering objects everywhere displayed, the shape of Edith in its rich dress seated before her glass, and the face of Edith as the glass presented it to him; and he betook himself to his old chamber of cogitation, carrying away with him a vivid picture in his mind of all these things, and a rambling and unaccountable speculation (such as sometimes comes into a man's head) how they would all look when he saw them next.

For the rest, Mr Dombey was very taciturn, and very dignified, and very confident of carrying out his purpose; and remained so. (Chap. 40)

Both Mr and Mrs Dombey show more than one side here; neither is a 'flat character'. But Dickens cannot give adequate expression to Edith's indignation. It is not simply a question of changing taste, of a modern intolerance for old conventions. Dickens not only uses a convention of queenly feminine disdain; he momentarily abandons himself and his imagined situation to the vocabulary it employs and the visions it suggests.

He does the same thing with the management of the plot where it relates to Dombey's marriage – that is, he allows melodramatic conventions to sweep him along and to violate the sense of reality and mask the serious implications he has developed. Dombey's marriage is a potentially admirable turn in the plot; it puts his will to make all his relationships serve his sense of his own greatness to a test more interesting than were any previous ones. Dombey has already been beaten twice, but beaten by the passive resistance of life to his requirements:

in the case of Paul, who could not stand up to his father's demands and died; in the case of Florence, who flourishes and wins all hearts despite his neglect and disfavour. Now, in Edith, he has for the first time an active, open opponent, someone as proud as he is and much more perceptive, someone who can articulately confront his assumption that his money makes him great. Accepting arbitrarily such a person's being willing to marry him, one has a situation which, however it may tempt to melodrama, has more than melodramatic potentialities. Edith is in a position to resist Dombey or to drive him to distraction. But (with one exception, Betsy Trotwood) Dickens will not let a good woman be effective in controversy. Given this arbitrary restriction on a character who cannot submit, the only remaining alternative is flight. Dickens has her flee with Carker.

Ever since Carker and Edith met, Dickens has been suggesting that their destinies are involved. Carker's original plot was to marry Florence and inherit the firm; when Edith came on the scene bearing the prospect of a new heir his attention naturally shifted to her. Running away with her is in some respects an appropriate dramatic climax of his plotting. From both Edith's and Carker's point of view it effectively humiliates Dombey; it is wicked and desperate: it fulfils the sense we have of Carker's cruel sensuality, which enjoys manœuvring proud women into positions in which submission to him entails their humiliation. It involves, however, Carker's sacrifice of the pursuit of money and power which has been his occupation. For Edith, flight with Carker, whom she hates and from whom she has a physical revulsion, seems improbable. The original plan – for her to become

his mistress and to die – is more arbitrary if less complicated and theatrical than its modification, according to
which she at least avoids him physically and punishes
his presumption. In the original plan her guilt in con-
senting to a marriage of 'interest and convenience'
(Carker's term) becomes swallowed up in the awful guilt
of adultery; in the event, she is not actually guilty but the
effect is retained of a catastrophe feeding her into the
mechanism of flight, pursuit, violence, Dombey's crash,
and separating her from the facts and motives of her
marriage.

The mechanism takes over Florence as well as Edith –
this catastrophe gives dramatic occasion to the outrage
which drives Florence out of Dombey's house and makes
possible her fairy tale rescue by Captain Cuttle and
Walter Gay. The blow which liberates Florence illustrates how Dickens's melodrama simultaneously knits
his story together, makes obeisance to social conventions,
weakens his characterization and frustrates his larger
goals. Dombey's violence, however plausible as the
frenzy of a man who has just discovered that his wife has
run off with his office manager, is uncharacteristic, a piece
of machinery put in to justify unfilial conduct – to place
him not only morally, but, so to speak, legally in the
wrong. Florence comes back in a year. She still loves her
father; she begs his forgiveness; she says she knows her
duty better now. The blow is recognized as something
which did not change the situation she had always lived
with, but merely dramatized her father's desperation.

Dickens has planned and prepared for a final break-
through of Dombey's sense of guilt in his relation with
Florence and a final coming together with her. For this to

take place Florence must, like Cordelia, return to suc-
cour him from her own establishment; the disinterestedness of her constancy cannot be strongly enough
established unless she is independent of her father. To
achieve this independence in a girl of seventeen is a nice
problem of plot. Clearly she must be under the protec-
tion of someone not her father. But she cannot have a
society wedding – she must go dowerless into the world.
Practically this means she must elope or flee by herself.
Eloping is a calculated act of disloyalty and as such
beneath Florence. Thus Dickens needs the aimless,
desperate, unplanned flight, and needs Dombey's
fantastic failure to do anything to recover his daughter –
even to find out where she is or whether she is still alive.
There must be a fierce crisis in Dombey's domestic
affairs to bring on such an aberration of his sense of what
is fitting in his family. Florence could not, by herself,
furnish such a crisis, and Edith is most convenient for it.
Thus there is a logical plot connection, working through
the blow Dombey strikes his daughter, between Edith's
flight with Carker and the reconciliation between
Dombey and Florence which Dickens has counted on
for the end of his novel.

Dickens's plot is all of a piece, despite the sketchiness
of the original plan and its alterations and accretions.
The marriage which comes to dominate the plot does
not strain it but gives it vigour and interest; the set scenes
into which the representation of the marriage and its
sequel fall do not, like the big scene in *Martin Chuzzlewit*,
wrench the story out of shape and dissipate its meaning.
The failure is not of the coherence of the plot itself; it is
rather that the working out of the plot seems to require

a faltering of characterization. Through their 'marriage of interest and convenience' Edith and Dombey are put in positions which Dickens cannot manage without inconsistency in their characters and, in her case, reliance on conventional stereotypes. In the character of Edith Dickens attempts a proud and perceptive woman intensely conscious of having sold herself – a challenging subject and the most ambitious use so far of his obsession with mercenary marriage. A combination of the demands of the plot, concessions to the powerful conventions surrounding the subject, and his own taste for lurid theatre wastes her potential as a character, and one finishes with her wondering why she couldn't have gone off and lived with Cousin Feenix in the first place. In the case of Dombey, Dickens is led by his plot to depart from essential attributes of character. Dombey's pride implies rigid adherence to standards of honour, propriety, and decency as he understands them. As Carker observes, his understanding of standards is obscured by his ego; still, his violation of these standards in the sequel of Edith's escape is too blatant.

A more fundamental objection can be made to the effect of Dombey's marriage in the novel. If, seeking to judge *Dombey and Son*'s successes and failures, one compares it to a work with a similar theme, *King Lear*, one sees immediately that a major weakness in Dickens's novel is the relative failure of Dombey to command sympathy and respect. With his frustrated, inept relations toward his son and daughter we can sympathize. But in his relationship with Edith he loses all stature; he is not only fatuous, he is mean and small. He fights her with dirty weapons – if she does not submit he will make

Florence suffer; he will send Carker, whom he knows she despises, with complaints and commands. Presumably Dickens put these meannesses into the story in order sufficiently to justify Edith's disobedience and flight, just as he had Dombey strike Florence in order to justify hers. But it seems also as if something in Dickens's values and attitudes would not allow a man who had made a cold and calculated marriage to keep his dignity even on his own terms. In reducing Dombey, Dickens undoes his own purposes. In *Bleak House*, dealing with a marriage of considerable similarity, Dickens did not make this mistake again; the novel gains in depth and power from the enforced recognition at its end of Sir Leicester Dedlock's qualities.

CHAPTER III

David Copperfield and *Bleak House*

AFTER *Dombey and Son* and before *Bleak House* comes *David Copperfield*, Dickens's 'favourite child' and a book which has always claimed a category of its own among his novels. One reason for its singularity as well as its popularity is its comparative lack of concern with social reform. This lack is not just a question of Dickens's failure to make a sustained attack on an institution (such as equity jurisprudence, administration, or parish relief), or to call attention to the sufferings of the poor. These omissions are found in other novels – for instance, *Dombey and Son* and *Great Expectations*. But in all the rest of Dickens's novels from *Oliver Twist* through *Our Mutual Friend* there is the sense that society is pervaded by ruthless egotism and needs a radical moral reformation. *David Copperfield*, despite the Murdstones, Creakle, Steerforth, Uriah Heep and his mother, lacks this sense. Except in the early episode of David's conflict with the Murdstones, the emphasis is on the need for personal discipline, not on the need for *caritas*.

This shift in orientation is reflected in the marriages which make up the plot. In earlier novels a bad marriage was a mercenary one, characteristically forced on young people by their calculating elders; in *Copperfield* most of the bad marriages are disinterested, innocent, and impulsive, while the good marriages – Peggotty's to

Barkis, Annie's to Dr Strong, David's to Agnes – are passionless and carefully weighed.

The Strongs furnish the most striking example of prudent marriage. Doctor Strong is old and rich, Annie is young and poor. Annie's mother is anxious to show Annie how useful her husband's money can be among her numerous relations (one is entitled to suspect a thrust at Mrs Hogarth), and implies frequently that the Doctor's generosity compensates for his age. Dickens suggests that Annie is attracted to her handsome cousin, Jack Maldon, and that her early love for him has been suppressed by the interested motives of her family. But early appearances turn out to have been deceiving. Jack Maldon is in fact the equivalent of David's Dora in her life, the menace of a phase she outgrew. In Dickens's plans for Numbers VI, VII, XII, XIV and XV is the evidence of how he calculated to associate Annie's situation with David's relation to Dora and to Agnes.* In Chapter 45 (No. XV) the true story comes out: Annie's marriage to Dr Strong has saved her from 'the first mistaken impulse of an undisciplined heart'. She would have been miserable with the flashy sponging Maldon – as she says, 'there can be no disparity in marriage like unsuitability of mind and purpose'. The phrases quoted are in the number plan and are repeated over and over again in the text. They are made to reflect upon David's increasing uneasiness and dissatisfaction with his own marriage.

Central to Dickens's treatment of the growth of David's character and the development of his self-knowledge is the theme of the undisciplined heart. This theme

* These number plans are reproduced in Butt and Tillotson, *Dickens at Work*, pp. 114-76.

is not, however, confined to David and Annie Strong; it pervades the novel. David's father and aunt have married unwisely for love; David's mother plunges fatuously into marriage with Murdstone; David himself marries a helpless child very like his mother. On the one hand are wilful passion, enthusiasm, fancy, romance; on the other hand are common sense and worldly wisdom expressed in a prudent marriage. David has several names which express this opposition. To his aunt he is Trotwood, renamed after his firm and sensible sister, Betsy Trotwood Copperfield, whom Aunt Betsy intended to bring up to avoid her own errors – 'There must be no mistakes in life with *this* Betsy Trotwood'). Agnes calls him 'Trot'. To Steerforth he is 'Daisy', the innocent and romantic hero-worshipper; to Dora he is 'Doady', terrifying unless he can be kept in the position of a playmate and doting lover-father. The stories not only of the Strongs but of most of the characters ancillary to David's career fit into the same pattern of oppositions. Little Emily runs away from a safe marriage with solid Ham Peggotty to pursue her dream of warm bright lands, blue seas, charm, distinction, passion and eventual fine gifts for Uncle Peggotty.* Micawber's romantic enthusiasm is part of his moral irresponsibility. Himself a rash breeder, the worst thing he does is to involve Traddles and Traddles's prudent matrimonial intentions in his money troubles – the furniture which Traddles and Sophy have been slowly accumulating for their household is seized and sold for Micawber's debts.

* Presumably Emily is in love with Steerforth in a way in which she is not in love with Ham. Dickens, to whom romantic love does represent a moral value, avoids implying any moral justification for Emily's action by muffling this aspect of the contrast between Steerforth and Ham.

The exceptions to this pattern are the stories of Uriah Heep and of the Murdstones, which follow much more closely the accustomed lines of Dickens's preoccupation with forced and mercenary marriage, but which emphaaize the element of personal aggression and violation rather then that of general corruption in society. Heep is a clear-cut reversion to an earlier melodramatic theme; in the classic style of a Gride or Quilp (but with the new twist of fake humility) he plots to impose his nasty self on Agnes Wickfield, who is to be forced into marrying him to save her father from financial ruin and exposure. The relation of Heep to Agnes is almost exactly the same as that of Pecksniff to Mary Graham, the difference being that Heep's plottings are far more effectual; he really has the girl's guardian under his thumb, while Pecksniff only thinks he has. We noted how, when Pecksniff becomes a sexual threat to Mary, he is seen vividly as a physical presence for the first time. Dickens makes sexual relationships real only when they are horrible to contemplate; thus by a kind of irony the forced or mercenary marriages — especially the ones which fail to come off — have in his readers' imaginations far more reality than the consummated loves of Nicholas or Young Martin or Walter Gay. With Uriah the imagined horror is carried to an extreme. For Agnes, his most abstractly perfect heroine, Dickens has prepared his most hideous and most tangibly physical menace. George Orwell's comment, 'It is the thought of the "pure" Agnes in bed with a man who drops his aitches that really revolts Dickens',* is at the same time revealing and misleading;

* George Orwell, 'Charles Dickens', *Dickens, Dali and Others* (New York, 1946), p. 41.

69

Heep's intentions certainly suggest pictures ('The image of Agnes, outraged by so much as a thought of this red-headed animal's, remained in my mind'), but Heep's social class is less relevant to their effect than his cold moist skin and the way he writhes.

Heep, then, is in intention a kind of rapist; one who hopes to accomplish the rape through economic pressure. Largely due to his physical presence, the bargain he means to strike with Agnes has a rawness about it lacking in, say, Mr Dombey's bargain with Edith. This overt physical violation is clearly one of the aspects of mercenary marriage which held Dickens's imagination and which made it a dramatic, even a compelling subject in itself and as a representation of aggression and violation in general. The melodramatic stereotypes of Gride gloating over Madeline's ripe red lips and Pecksniff imprisoning Mary's delicate hand are meant to express a lurid form of the will to power over others – the will which Dickens sees at the heart of the evil in society. Uriah Heep as a representative of this evil stands somewhere in between the crudeness of Quilp and the dark complexity of Mrs Clennam and Miss Havisham. He is noteworthy not only in the extreme to which Dickens pushes the physical element in his intentions, but also in the ironic inversion which expresses his demonic drive in terms of humility.

Murdstone, no less extreme an exponent of the will to dominate and control, is simpler and less devious. Although there is some ambiguity about his reason for marrying (his last marriage brings him a 'very good little property') he seems a fairly straightforward sadist. He marries David's mother not, evidently, for her money (all she has is the house and an annuity of a hundred and five pounds a year), but for the pleasure of crushing her. This pleasure is not quite pure; it seems to be mixed with some affection and some regret.*

Monstrously swollen with spiritual pride, Murdstone has plenty of self-discipline and prudence when he needs it to carry out his ends. Like Heep, he is not involved in the theme of the undisciplined heart. Except from the point of view of David's mother (a point of view no more than Dora's taken into account in the novel), he has not even a tangential relation to the pattern of imprudence in following first impulses. Murdstone is not a particularly useful figure in the novel from the standpoint of its hero's moral education. One can make him relate interestingly to David's development only by going beyond what seem to be Dickens's intentions to speculate upon the striking similarity between Murdstone's relation to Mrs Copperfield and David's to Dora.

Dickens means us to see that Dora is very like David's mother, but he thinks of the parallel as one between David and his father, not his stepfather. But both stepfather and stepson are distressed by their wives' lack of firmness; both put moral pressure on them to reform. Both wives feel guilty for being what they are; both die. The little boy David, encumbrance and object of foolish devotion, finds a parallel in the little dog Gyp, who must be extravagantly provided for and who furnishes an

---

* It will be remembered that Jonas Chuzzlewit married Mercy Pecksniff for somewhat similar reasons. Murdstone's relation to his bride represents a considerable advance in psychological sophistication. Unlike Jonas, he cannot admit openly or even understand his own intentions; unlike Jonas he cannot explain or justify his conduct by the torment his bride inflicted on him before they were married.

irritating distraction from serious business and self-improvement.

David's mother's death is explicitly blamed on the Murdstones (by Betsy Trotwood, whose word may be taken). It is made an occasion of real sorrow, more real through the evocation of the child's sense of importance, the undertaker's jollity, the love-making going on in the wagon which carries the coffin. In contrast, Dora's death is thoroughly unreal, something to be got over, with appropriate gestures, as quickly as possible.

Dickens builds up as much as he can manage of the hushed and sorrowful anticipation to which he has accustomed his readers as the aura of a thoroughly regrettable death. But there is no attempt to avoid the contradictory implication that Dora's death is in effect a providential release for David. What is avoided is any suggestion that he is psychologically guilty. David is shown accepting her limitations and doing his best to make her feel her own worth. He is made to accept his inability to reform her. Aunt Betsy, who calls Dora 'Little Blossom', refuses to try to help teach her to be practical, and a mood of conscious tenderness and tolerance for her weakness is thrown over all around her. It is clear to all, however, that the best thing Dora can do is to die, to become an educational episode in David's life instead of a disastrous mistake which will permanently blight it. Here is Dora on her death bed:

'Oh, Doady, after more years, you never could have loved your child-wife better than you do; and after more years, she would so have tried and disappointed you that you might not have been able to love her half so well! I know I was too young and foolish. It is much better as it is!' (Chap. 53).

Dickens does not kill Dora gratuitously – one does not need to search in Dickens's own experience for reasons for her death. The intention of his book leaves him no choice; if *David Copperfield* is to be a novel of education, Dora must die. A *Bildungsroman* cannot allow fatal mistakes which close the protagonists' prospect into the future and render useless what he has learned.

But in his attempts to deal with unpleasant implications of the obvious fact that Dora's death is a providential escape for David, Dickens aggravates the problem of getting rid of her. Dora's willingness to give up life in order to avoid becoming a drag on her husband or a disappointment to him ('It is better as it is') is a terrible indictment of David, as well as of the mind that could conceive of such a thing without seeing it a monstrosity. If we could take Dora's final statements seriously – her expressed desire to get out of her husband's way, her invitation to Agnes to marry him – then we would have to see David as a man who has been unable to avoid convincing his wife that her death will be a stroke of good fortune to him. But we cannot – it is all quite unreal. Dickens is merely ashamed of doing away with Dora for his hero's convenience and is trying to make it nicer by having her show understanding and willingness to go along – rather like making a hanging nicer by emphasizing the understanding and co-operation of the victim.

Even after one allows for distortions like this, caused by factors external to Dickens's conception of David's character; even admitting as unmeaning coincidence the parallel circumstances of their wives' deaths, there remain important similarities between Murdstone and David. At the end of the book David is not much like any

73

of Dickens's other heroes. He is a successful man whose climb to success has been made real and important, and has been convincingly explained by the qualities of energy and steely determination. The dramatic reality of David's climb is partly due, of course, to the half-autobiographical nature of the book – David makes a success of himself in the only way Dickens really knew.

But in other novels, not only is Dickens ignorant of and uninterested in the processes by which his heroes make their livelihoods, he is really uninterested in their economic success, which he makes arbitrary and improbable. Most of the good people in Dickens are not capable of being successes in a world based on money, and their incapability partly defines their goodness. All discerning readers of *The Pickwick Papers* have realized how extremely unlikely it is for Pickwick to have made even a modest fortune in business; the same is true, if not, perhaps, as glaringly, of the other rich benevolent business men in Dickens.

The character of Mr Pickwick, an elderly child and the archetypal Dickensian hero, has important relevance to *David Copperfield*, a novel about growing up. Pickwick has the spontaneity, the simplicity, the undirected gaity of the ideal boy. His heart, as Sam Weller points out, was born many years later than his body. Romping in the snow at Dingley Dell, he represents a triumph of boyish exuberance over time. Pickwick's innocence and enthusiasm are such that he needs an adult person, a Sam Weller, to take him about and protect his interests. David, as he ceases to be Steerforth's Daisy, as his will, determination, and confidence come more and more to the fore, grows further and further from this Pickwickian spontaneity and innocence. But Murdstone is Pickwick's real opposite. Work, will, achievement, success, these are the demands the Murdstones make and accept; they have built their lives around abstract imperatives.

'Never be mean in anything; never be false; never be cruel,' says Aunt Betsy to David. These are abstract imperatives, but of a type different from Murdstone's, at least in Dickens's psychology, which awards generosity, truth, and kindness as natural virtues inherent and spontaneous to Smikes and Swivellers and Tootses. Murdstone's imperatives are consciously held in straining tension against the flow of experience; Murdstone's will to uphold them is implicit in everything he does. This is what makes him so terrifying to children. A child does not begin to understand Murdstone, but he recognizes his will to enforce submission; he knows Mr Murdstone is out to break David, even though this makes no sense. A child understands immediately that it is Murdstone's principle to be pitiless, and that Murdstone's principles are absolute. He knows that Murdstone will do what he says he will do, no matter how horrible.

From *Nicholas Nickleby* on, all Dickens's major villains share Murdstone's dedication to abstractions; all have stern wills, and almost all are intensely anxious to get ahead; most, like Ralph Nickleby, or Pecksniff, or Dombey are loyal to their principles and to their abstract ambitions when such loyalty is clearly ruinous. The attractive characters are those who take no heed for the morrow. Even the relatively earnest and colourless young heroes – Nicholas, Young Martin, Edward Chester, Walter Gay – depend on lucky accidents to get ahead;

the Micawber faith in 'something turning up' is justified in them.

David, then, is a new kind of Dickens hero, one who develops some of the grim confidence, method, and will hitherto reserved to Dickens's villains. The similarity suggests speculation along the biographical lines of Edmund Wilson's essay. Dickens himself, however much he admires Pickwick and shares with him traits of kindness, gusto, high spirits, and generous indignation, has also clear affinities to Pickwick's opposite, Murdstone. The scheme of values which discredits his own fierce will and aggression could be difficult to sustain in a novel about a young man who is to achieve a similar success by similar discipline of will and energy. In fact we find that it is not sustained.

Pickwick devotes himself to pursuing and unmasking the heiress-hunter Jingle, combating Mrs Bardell's conspiracy, and promoting the disinterested loves of his young friends; David devotes himself to getting ahead and to fulfilling the responsibilities he has incurred. The problem in Pickwick's world, as in the world of most of Dickens's novels, is to protect men and women from combinations of private greed and bad institutions; the problem in David's world is to protect men and women from their own imprudent impulses and foolish dreams. In the first world people are menaced by forced or mercenary marriages; in the second by imprudent ones.

Psychologically the two worlds are closely related to each other: as the pressures of adulthood in a competitive society drive one towards conceiving of one's world as David comes to do, one yearns to conceive of it as Pickwick does. But if a man acts with Pickwick's generosity, enthusiasm, and unselfishness he accumulates responsibilities and pressures. What brings out David's fierce and disciplined will is his commitment to Dora – in itself something spontaneous, 'the first mistaken impulse of an undisciplined heart'. As he steels himself to hack a way through the forest of difficulties to Dora he develops at the same time a hard will and a need for rest and nurture less and less suited both to her character and to their relation as he had originally conceived it.* He begins to scorn the original conception as something childish and unrealistic.

David regrets his growing tiredness and wishes he had a wife who could take better care of him. It seems justifiable to assume that Dickens, regretting his own fatigue and prizing the freshness and spontaneity he celebrates in Pickwick, understands that the erosion of these qualities and their replacement by dogged devotion to the principle of aggrandizement is related to marriage and the support of a family. Pickwick is a free man with no hostages to fortune, a traveller with light baggage. When one starts to collect impedimenta and children this freedom disappears along with the Pickwickian innocence. This is a truism, but not one whose implications Dickens could find easy to accept. For one thing, it runs counter to his attempt to sustain a belief in ideal romantic love and marriage. It links the cosy little domestic refuge to the radical and anarchic selfishness

---

* It is important to notice that David comes to object to Dora not as an inadequate intellectual companion but as a bad housewife; what weighs upon him is not her dullness but the disorder, discomfort and expense of his household. In this respect, see Edgar Johnson, *Charles Dickens, His Tragedy and Triumph* (New York, 1952), II, 905-8. Catherine Dickens's housekeeping ineptitude evidently grated terribly on Dickens.

and cruelty of his society. It admits into men's affairs a determinism, a suggestion of human helplessness to make good intentions and honest determination bear good fruit, which is totally alien to Dickens's point of view. Perhaps mercenary marriage is in part a kind of metaphor to dramatize the erosion of what is spontaneous and loving by the aggrandizement principle which can occur when one marries and founds a family, and at the same time to separate this erosion from the spontaneous and disinterested love relations which Dickens's romanticism demanded. In *David Copperfield*, where his subject forced him closer to his own life, this separation breaks down, and we see the development of a romantic lover into a fiercely ambitious novelist, we see a generous and unselfish young man working ceaselessly to support a new establishment, increasingly impatient with his wife, eventually accepting sadly but with unsuccessfully disguised satisfaction the death she willingly dies to gratify him.

David's comfort and success require his wife's life; Dickens muffles and mitigates as much as he can the cruelty and selfishness of this requirement. But there remains a moral embarrassment, a palpable conflict between common sense and decency. After *David Copperfield* Dickens always insists that his good marriages be not only disinterested but also without regrets or afterthoughts. And he does not allow any characters after David to survive their mistakes in love or marriage relatively undamaged. Unhappy involvements – Lady Dedlock's, Louisa Gradgrind's, Miss Havisham's, Pip's – must ultimately be terribly expiated. *David Copperfield*, in its concern with personal success as well as with prudence and the disciplined heart, is a holiday not only from Dickens's social concerns, but from his usual moral insistences.

In *Bleak House* Dickens returns with far more organized detail and force to his examination of the condition of England and to his plea for reform. As he does so his emphasis shifts back from prudent marriages to pointedly disinterested ones – Ada's, Esther's (arranged by Mr Jarndyce as an act of ultimate generosity), Caddy's. At the centre of the plot, Lady Dedlock has married for money and position, concealing an obscure and disreputable episode with a young officer.

Lady Dedlock's high position will be forfeit, on moral grounds, if her secret is discovered, but according to the implicit moral values of the novel, her secret is less censurable than the life she has chosen in marrying Sir Leicester. Thus Lady Dedlock's guilt is ambiguous. She has been unchaste, passionate, foolish – a veritable Lydia Bennet to Captain Hawdon's Wilkins.* She has then recovered from her mistake with a marriage excellent from many standpoints, but, as Dickens makes clear, deeply wrong for her. Sir Leicester is in some respects an admirable husband; his steady gallantry, loyalty, and true love for his lady must be allowed to compensate somewhat for his age and dullness. Let us remember Dr Strong and Jack Maldon! – Lady Dedlock has indeed been rescued from 'the first mistaken impulse of an undisciplined heart' and solidly established with a good old

---

* The Victorian Dickens is consistently more tender toward illicit sex and unwed motherhood than one could be in Regency fiction.

man who loves her. But the values are all different. Annie Strong's characteristic posture is on her knees, helping the old Doctor with his boots or weeping because she feels unworthy of him; Lady Dedlock sits at her ease on the other side of the fire and tosses a jewelled fan. She is immensely successful in a world Dickens scorns – '. . . for years now, my Lady Dedlock has been at the centre of the fashionable intelligence and at the top of the fashionable tree.' Dickens suggests that she achieved these positions deliberately, and that her marriage was ancillary to her ambition: 'she had beauty, pride, ambition, insolent resolve and sense. . . . Wealth, and station added to these, soon floated her upward.' Her boredom is the result of achieved ambition – 'My Lady Dedlock, having conquered *her* world, fell not into the melting but rather into the freezing mood' (Chap. 2). By marrying Sir Leicester, Lady Dedlock has choked her own life; now she lives on without interest, tenderness, or enthusiasm.

The discovery of Captain Hawdon, and the stirring up of a mystery around his old relations with Lady Dedlock shows us (and reminds her) of what she was once capable, makes her realize what she has lost by her choice of life, and puts the Dedlocks and Chesney Wold in a larger perspective. But the discovery and the mystery is presented to us, with all Dickens's gusto in hunting down criminals, as an occasion for detective work in ferreting out a hidden sin; in this context Lady Dedlock's guilt in going to bed with Captain Hawdon and in deceiving Sir Leicester (presumably he thought she was a virgin) is made to take precedence over her guilt in marrying for money and position.

Edmund Wilson discusses *Bleak House* as an example

of a new genre – 'the detective story that is also a social fable'. According to Wilson, 'The solution of the mystery is also the moral of the story and the last word in Dickens's social "message" '.* But this formula does not work with *Bleak House*, at least not in the straightforward way Wilson's language suggests. The moral of the book is not directly stated in the solution of its two mysteries.†

This moral has nothing to do with the idea that sexual irregularity is always punished in the end or that rich glamorous people can have disreputable pasts, but a great deal to do with the idea that the highest and haughtiest are intimately linked to the poorest and most desperate. At the end of all Mr Bucket's detective work, after the solution of all mysteries, Lady Dedlock will be found dead in Jenny's ragged dress outside the gate of the rat-infested slum graveyard where her lover lies less than a foot underground; she will then be 'entombed' in the Dedlock 'mausoleum' at Chesney Wold. A leader of the 'fashionable world', whose portrait, in the 'Galaxy gallery of British beauty', stands on Mr Weevle's‡ mantleshelf, she is driven to seek the aid of Jo, Jenny and Guster (the Snagsbys' epileptic servant), three of the most downtrodden people in England. We are all involved with each other – this is the 'social message' of the

---

* Edmund Wilson, 'Dickens, The Two Scrooges', *The Wound and the Bow* (New York, 1947), p. 36.

† There is a minor mystery – requiring even more dramatic detective work – which deals with the question of who shot Mr Tulkinghorn. Aside from the, no doubt, useful lessons that it is unwise to insult passionate Southerners and that no arrogance is safe from desperate violence, there is no moral to be drawn from the solution of this mystery.

‡ Mr Weevle's real name, as Mr Guppy says, is Jobling.

book, enforced likewise through the web of Chancery and the contagion of smallpox.

This moral is less directly involved with the mystery of what Mr Chadband calls Lady Dedlock's 'sinful secret' than with the arbitrary and accidental circumstances of her lover's life after she lost sight of him. It is Captain Hawdon's poverty and squalid death which lead to her dealings with the wretchedness of Tom-all-Alone's. Captain Hawdon's circumstances are irrelevant to the vital elements of Dickens's detective story – to Lady Dedlock's past, to her own conflicting values and motives, to the values and motives of those seeking to expose her or protect her. The tension and suspense of Tulkinghorn's and Guppy's detective work, the drama of Lady Dedlock's imprisonment in her high situation, of the contrast between her self-command and her yearning after her dead lover and lost child – all these lack a clear relation to the circumstances which make her figure the involvement of the highest and lowest of society. What gives body and interest to the mystery, what makes it important to the people involved in it, seems to have only a tangential connection with what makes it support the main moral of the story.

But this is only true if one understands Lady Dedlock's guilt as unchastity before marriage and Mr Tulkinghorn's motive as zeal to expose this sexual impurity and cut it away from the Dedlocks. If one understands her real sin as that of marrying for money and position instead of for love the connection between the mystery of Lady Dedlock's past and the moral of the novel becomes much firmer and more logical; the squalor of Tom-all-Alone's and its hideous graveyard comes to

have a valid symbolic relation to the choice Lady Dedlock made when she sinned.

There is a tension here between conventional values –
presumably the values of Dickens's readers, which he
accepted at least nominally himself – and the standards
which really count in the novel. This tension is most
evident in the presentation of Mr Tulkinghorn's
motives. Lady Dedlock's youthful offence against conventional morality makes her vulnerable, but it does not
adequately explain Mr Tulkinghorn's decision to hunt
her down and then to expose her. Dickens suggests
various unsatisfactory explanations but reveals the true
one. We are told that Mr Tulkinghorn is a man who
likes to find out important family secrets. But such an
explanation through an arbitrary ruling passion does not
explain why the lawyer should intend to use his secret to
destroy Lady Dedlock. Dickens implies that Mr
Tulkinghorn really resents the Dedlocks' overwhelming
pride and means to humble them;* it is difficult, however, to accept such a solid, discreet and self-respecting
family lawyer as deliberately and spitefully working
against his client's interest. The true explanation seems
to be that Mr Tulkinghorn considers Lady Dedlock a
kind of intruder, that he senses her incompatibility with
her husband's family and her unfitness for her position –
an unfitness arising not from her youthful impurity, but
from her capacity for passionate love and commitment,
from her ultimate dissatisfaction with the values and life
of the Dedlock family.

* 'That was a hypothetical case, arising out of Sir Leicester unconsciously carrying
the matter with so high a hand' (Chap. 41), says Tulkinghorn when Lady Dedlock
asks him whether Rosa's friends know the secret and are ashamed of Rosa's connection
with her.

When Lady Dedlock and Mr Tulkinghorn finally confront one another, Mr Tulkinghorn makes it plain that he intends to use his information to separate her from her husband, but not, if possible, to raise a scandal. To Mr Tulkinghorn the danger is that Sir Leicester may be loyal to his wife despite everything. Speaking to Lady Dedlock of Sir Leicester's 'infatuation' with her, he says:

He might not be able to overcome that infatuation, even knowing what we know. I am putting an extreme case, but it might be so. If so, it were better that he know nothing. Better for common sense, better for him, better for me. (Chap 41)

Evidently Sir Leicester's health, life, and sanity are secondary in his lawyer's scheme of values to other aspects of his person: 'This is to be hushed up if it can be. How can it be if Sir Leicester is driven out of his wits, or laid upon a deathbed?' Mr Tulkinghorn explains in this scene what he means by 'Sir Leicester':

'When I speak of Sir Leicester being the sole consideration, he and the family credit are one. Sir Leicester and the baronetcy, Sir Leicester and Chesney Wold, Sir Leicester and his ancestors and his patrimony.' – Mr Tulkinghorn very dry here – 'are, I need not say to you, Lady Dedlock, inseparable.' (Chap. 41)

Sir Leicester's self-importance indicates that he shares this view; he evidently considers himself an institution, part of the British Constitution. His redeeming flaw is expressed in his relationship with Lady Dedlock; as Dickens says, 'he married her for love'. And 'his gallantry to my Lady, which has never changed since he courted her, is the one little touch of romantic fancy about him' (Chap. 2). Mr Tulkinghorn's vendetta against Lady Dedlock becomes completely intelligible if it is seen as his attempt to make Sir Leicester, from his point of view, perfect.

Mr Tulkinghorn is himself perfect in his kind; in him Dickens presents a representative as extreme in one way as Pecksniff is in another of an approach to life which organizes all relations and regulates all values to protect and extend personal comfort, power, and position. Mercenary marriage is for such persons in Dickens the characteristic field of operation, and it is no surprise to learn that Mr Tulkinghorn 'is reputed to have made good thrift out of aristocratic marriage settlements and aristocratic wills'. Sir Leicester, with his romantic gallantry and loyalty, is not allowed to stand for his class in this area of his relative attractiveness. Dickens invokes the figure of Volumnia Dedlock to assert the connection between mercenary marriage and the aristocracy. At the end of the chapter in which he confronts Lady Dedlock with Mr Tulkinghorn, Dickens specifically contrasts class attitudes towards marriage:

The same wan day peeps in for Sir Leicester, pardoning the country in a majestically condescending dream; and at the cousins entering upon various public employments, principally receipt of salary; and at the chaste Volumnia, bestowing a dower of fifty thousand pounds upon a hideous old General, with a mouth of false teeth like a pianoforte too full of keys, long the admiration of Bath and the terror of every other community. Also into rooms high in the roof, and into offices in the courtyards and over stables, where humbler ambition dreams of bliss, in keeper's lodges, and in holy matrimony with Will or Sally. (Chap. 41)

Dickens's anxiety to make his point has here led him into unfairness and absurdity; everyone but Volumnia is allowed to dream of something conceivably most desirable to him. Volumnia is not even allowed to dream of getting youth and beauty as well as distinction for her money.

Mr Tulkinghorn, then, is the guardian of the standards in marriage exemplified by Volumnia, which Sir Leicester, in the one eccentricity of his life, has violated. Seeing him as such a guardian, one can make sense of his otherwise arbitrary and unjustified claim that Lady Dedlock has broken her agreement with him by dismissing Rosa; their clash over Rosa puts in perspective the entire struggle between them. Mr Tulkinghorn, who has witnessed the dismissal, understands that Lady Dedlock means to save Rosa from involvement in her own shame, and claims that her action shows she is not to be trusted; he tells her that he now intends to 'undeceive' Sir Leicester without further notice. Lady Dedlock has not (as Mr Tulkinghorn asserts) given any possible occasion for rumour in her manner of dismissing Rosa, and Mr Tulkinghorn's statement that she has been 'transparently' different from what she was before is false. But it contains a truth; under an effective disguise she has done something uncharacteristic – she has gone out of her way to be kind; she has exerted herself to help a village girl marry an ironmaster's son. Although she has not compromised Mr Tulkinghorn's secret in any way, Lady Dedlock has given him further evidence of the streak in her which he suspected from the first, which made her capable of generosity, passion, sacrifice, disinterested love, and which has been more and more evident as he has continued to press on her.* In the deepest sense, Tulkinghorn is true to what he represents when he lets Lady Dedlock's action toward Rosa determine him to destroy her.

Lady Dedlock is likewise true to herself; she finally uses her pride and high resolve to defend the decent values her position has so long denied her. She defies Mr Tulkinghorn: 'Nothing in the world, and no one in the world ... could move me'. The interest that Lady Dedlock takes in Rosa and her resolve to make the girl happy are a response to her awakened memories of the episode with Captain Hawdon, and of her own lost little girl. Rosa gives her a chance to live vicariously, to help someone avoid her own mistakes. Rosa is involved in every stage of the struggle between the lawyer and Lady Dedlock.

We know little about Rosa – only that she is a village girl, nineteen years old, pretty, shy, humble, malleable, devoted to Lady Dedlock and in love with Watt Rouncewell.† Mr Rouncewell, the ironmaster, who admits that people of his class are usually disappointed when their sons marry factory girls, claims nevertheless that 'unequal' marriages are not uncommon in the industrial districts, and has proposed to put Rosa to school to make her fit for his son. Sir Leicester's indignation at the idea

* 'As to sparing the girl, of what importance of value is she? Spare! Lady Dedlock, here is a family name compromised. One might have supposed that the course was straight on – over everything, neither to the right nor to the left, regardless of all considerations in the way, sparing nothing, treading everything under foot.' (Chap. 48)

† 'Watt' has a double significance; Sir Leicester identifies all threats to the political and social order with Wat Tyler. At one point when Mr Rouncewell refers to his son Dickens spells it 'Wat.' Two pages before, Sir Leicester has feared that there may be 'a hidden Wat Tylerish meaning' in one of Mr Rouncewell's expressions. (Chap. 48)

that Rosa is to be equated with factory girls and that two years in a school for manufacturers' daughters could recommend her better than his lady's patronage, has determined Mr Rouncewell to oppose the marriage. By writing to the ironmaster and asking him to take Rosa and go through with his project Lady Dedlock has subverted her husband's values, especially those which he attaches to the splendour and pride of her position. Rosa's eventual marriage to Watt will represent a posthumous triumph for Lady Dedlock and a defeat for Mr Tulkinghorn; it is ironic but symbolically right that she should achieve this victory by ostentatiously cutting Rosa away from her own person and example.

Lady Dedlock salvages from her own destruction a love marriage for her surrogate daughter. Her real daughter, whom she cannot help, is similarly provided for by others. Esther's marriage is elaborately contrived as an exercise in disinterestedness. Both Esther and her husband are extremely poor, and Esther's beauty has been destroyed by smallpox. Mr Jarndyce's benevolence is necessary to bring the two together. Jarndyce has asked Esther to marry him, but only after her face has been scarred and he knows she is cast down over her illegitimacy.* When Woodcourt returns from the East, Jarndyce soon sees that Esther must marry him, and goes to work to arrange a house and grounds for them and to convince Woodcourt's pedigree-obsessed mother that Esther is a jewel. A triangle is set up in which all three principals, recognizing their own limitations, are willing to sacrifice their dearest wishes to the good of

* She is evidently worrying about the predictions her aunt made about her — see Chapter 44.

others. Esther's natural humility, reinforced by her sense
that she is disfigured and that her lineage is tainted, for-
bids her aspiring to the man she really wants — further,
she feels she owes her duty to her guardian, who seems
to need her as a wife. Woodcourt's sense of his poverty
and of Jarndyce's greater claims evidently inhibits his
courtship; he accepts without argument Esther's statement that she is already taken. Jarndyce, who is in a
position to endow the other two and to overcome their
generous scruples, knows that his age is a decisive disability which puts poverty, illegitimacy and marred
beauty in their right perspective; furthermore, he understands that his role is not to have, but to give.

In *Bleak House*, then, for the next to the last time*
Dickens uses a generous rich man who puts things right
with his money to make possible a disinterested marriage.
As has often been pointed out, Jarndyce is frustrated and
unsuccessful in his philanthropy to a degree unprece-
dented among Dickens's philanthropists — his world is
much darker and more complicated than that of the
Cheeryble brothers. Nevertheless his position and function toward Esther and Woodcourt have not advanced
beyond theirs toward Madeline and Nicholas. Dickens
still needs this simple, improbable figure, showering
guineas, because he stills wants his heroes and heroines
to have it both ways — to be pure and disinterested, but
also to settle in a little villa with 'tiny wooden colonnades,
garlanded with woodbine, jasmine and honeysuckle'
(Chap. 64) an apple and cherry orchard and, of course, a
small staff to keep the place up. If his young heroes and
heroines are to avoid any suspicion of marrying for

* The last generous rich man who does this is Boffin, in *Our Mutual Friend*.

money and yet to have these things (right away, after the wedding, without the grim and uncertain process of aggrandizement through the years) they need a fairy godfather.

The difference between the marriages in *Nicholas Nickleby* and the marriage of Esther Summerson lies not in the function of the rich old men in either case, but in the characters of the young people. In *Bleak House* Dickens has shown that he understands more deeply the implication of the idea of disinterestedness in marriage – the distinction it sets up between extrinsic and intrinsic qualities in persons. Esther is a bride not only without money and position but also without beauty or legitimacy; Dickens must enforce the value of her inner qualities. What has bothered perhaps most readers of *Bleak House* – the stream of evidence of Esther's transcendent goodness which flows from Esther's pen – is therefore essential. Dickens did not make Esther perfect out of perversity. He had a worthy purpose, to make a character who would show what he meant by disinterested love, who would drive home the distinction between inner worth and all respects of property, family, superficial beauty which lead men and women, in manipulating them and concentrating on them, to become hard and selfish. The failure of his purpose, the inadequacy of Esther to her role, can be best shown by contrast with Amy Dorrit in *Little Dorrit*.

Bleak House has, on the whole, a more tightly organized structure of plot, symbol, and meaning than *Little Dorrit*, but its use of mercenary marriage as a symbol of what is wrong in society is weaker. The difference between the two books in this latter respect is to a large extent a measure of the difference between Esther and Amy. The two girls play very similar roles; they exemplify what is opposed to the selfishness, false pride, jobbery, boredom, and waste reaching like a web through their society – they stand up for love, loyalty, unselfishness, and duty. But Esther, despite Dickens's earnest efforts, is not as effective in her part as Amy is; her relatively secure and protected situation does not allow her unselfishness scope, and her function as narrator conflicts with her function in the novel's system of symbol and meaning. She is rewarded for her virtue by a marriage heavily endowed (though elaborately disinterested) to a young man who is obviously put into the book to marry her. Like Arthur Clennam, Woodcourt is a selfless person, one who stands apart from the conniving of his society. But compared with Clennam he is a trivial and perfunctory figure. The effect of Esther's goodness is muffled by comparison with Amy's, and her marriage (unlike Amy's, which enhances her) reduces her to the level of a commonplace heroine, one inadequate to strike the note Dickens requires for the end of his great novel.

Little Dorrit ends with Arthur and Amy going down the church steps into a world inimical to their characters and values in ways the book has taught us to understand; *Bleak House* ends with a picture of Chesney Wold, of Volumnia proceeding to 'the exhausted old assembly room, fourteen heavy miles off', of the dead house, with no flag flying, where 'passion and pride have died away, even to the stranger's eye . . . and yielded it to dull repose'. Esther's last chapter presents her merely as observer, focusing not upon her happiness with Woodcourt but upon Richard Carstone's death (occasioned by the final absorption by legal costs of the whole estate in the case of Jarndyce and Jarndyce). Ada Carstone, who has been through most of the novel a mere cipher, seems a more considerable figure at the end than Esther; she has married Richard when his prospects were gone in order to struggle with Mr Vholes for his soul. She has lost, but her reckless and futile gesture dignifies her and enforces, as does the drama of Lady Dedlock, the relation of human passion and loyalty to the institutions and values Dickens is fighting.

CHAPTER IV

Little Dorrit

Little Dorrit has attracted an especially full share of the recent critical attention to metaphors, symbols and recurring images in Dickens's novels. In breaking away from the old tradition of not taking this novel seriously as an organized whole, critics have usually tried to assert the book's unity by emphasizing the pervasiveness in it of the metaphor of imprisonment. To see how this critical solution works one can look at Miss Wade's story, which, viewed in the light of this pervasive metaphor, is not a distraction but an integral part of the book and an important elucidation of its meaning. Being imprisoned by a neurosis is much the most effective and total curtailment of freedom, and this is true for Mr Dorrit and Mrs Clennam as well as for Miss Wade.

The sense of illumination fostered in this instance and others by noticing the unifying force of a metaphor should not be allowed to extend itself to matters that are not illuminated. The organization of *Little Dorrit* does not depend upon the metaphor of imprisonment, but upon the relation between two characters, Arthur Clennam and Amy Dorrit. Both are emblematic; both are set off against groups of other people. In the complex plot built around these characters Dickens's obsession with the relation between marriage and money and his criticism of the radical evil of selfish will in society are drawn

93

together with impressive skill and power. As human beings Arthur and Amy are only fitfully convincing, and their relation to each other loses some of its effect through the huddling in of essential plot connections at the end of the book. Thus the organization of *Little Dorrit* cannot be considered more than a limited success. But such as it is, it should be noticed.

In the second chapter of *Little Dorrit* (the first introduces Cavaletto and Rigaud in prison) we meet Arthur Clennam explaining his purposelessness to Mr Meagles:

'I have no will. That is to say,' – he coloured a little, – 'next to none that I can put in action now. Trained by main force; broken, not bent; heavily ironed with an object upon which I was never consulted and which was never mine; shipped away to the other end of the world before I was of age, and exiled there until my father's death there, a year ago; always grinding in a mill I always hated; what is to be expected from *me* in middle life? Will, purpose, hope? All those lights were extinguished before I could sound the words.'

'Light 'em up again!' said Mr Meagles.

Clennam is listless and discouraged because of his harsh and joyless upbringing and because he has been forced into a job he hates. In the course of the novel a number of further misfortunes keep his spirits low. Some are private afflictions – his bitter homecoming, the harsh light which meeting Flora Finching throws on his youth and his dreams, the disappointment of his love for Pet, the subtle cruelty of Henry Gowan. Some are more public; misfortunes in which he is a representative sufferer, like the frustration of his repeated efforts to find out or accomplish things through the Circumlocution Office, the loss of his money in the Merdle crash and his subsequent imprisonment in the Marshalsea. Resolute, patient, always defeated, Clennam is a perennial victim of the political and economic establishment of his country. A great deal of what is wrong in the complex of English religion, government, and finance seems to bear directly on him; on the other hand he is the friend and patron of those really crushed or maimed – Plornish, Cavaletto, William Dorrit.

It is useful to look at the alignment of forces in this novel, and to consider the implications of setting up Arthur Clennam at the focus of their opposition. One does not need a Marxist perspective to be tempted to see in *Little Dorrit* a simple confrontation: governing and money-making classes, rapacious and, on the whole, indolent, on one side; decent, bewildered, struggling poor on the other, with only an occasional eccentric mechanic or businessman like Doyce and Meagles, or honourable and sensitive gentlemen like Clennam to defend their interests. *Little Dorrit* has, of course, Shaw's testimonial for it as a revolutionary novel; if we are to accept as seriously meant – as we must – its picture of an England run by a coalition of Barnacles and Merdles, we must accept it as in some sense revolutionary. But the novel does not present to us an opposition between the oppressors and the oppressed. It is much less concerned with the miseries of the poor than either *Hard Times* or *Bleak House*. Although logically we must expect the tenants of Bleeding Heart Yard to suffer from the defects of their governors and of the political and economic system these governors maintain, we do not in fact see them suffer very much. Dickens enforces a vision of pride of place, self-will, inertia, anxiety, and concealment as dominating motives in the governing and propertied classes of his civilization; he is essentially concerned with the moral implications of these motives rather than the economic and political effects on the community. One senses that the latter are insisted on to strengthen the argument, to assert the importance of the subject. Certainly the tenants of Bleeding Heart Yard are not morally involved except in their admiration for Merdle. They figure as an abstract quantity, and as witnesses. They must watch Pancks cut off Casby's hair and hat brim; they do not know enough to do it themseves, and it would be wrong for them to try. In fact, although we know abstractly that Casby has been oppressing them, we see him oppress only Pancks. Casby and Pancks re-enact on a smaller scale the relation of Clennam and English institutions; the real weight of the Barnacles, the Circumlocution Office, the rotten financial system dominated and symbolized by Merdle, the dreadful Puritan Sunday, the systematic suppression of joy which people like Mrs Clennam carry out 'as part of a bargain for the security of their possessions', falls on Clennam. We are much more involved in his suffering than in the suffering of those whose interests he champions. He means to help Doyce, Meagles, and Amy Dorrit, but proves consistently powerless to do so; they, on the other hand, combine to save him at the end.

Clennam's two roles, then, are of champion of the oppressed, and of victim and sufferer; of the two the second is more important. If one examines what actually happens in the novel, one sees not a struggle between social forces with Clennam championing one of them, but an onslaught of social forces against Clennam, with Doyce, Meagles, and Little Dorrit working to protect and redeem him. Clennam is the *locus* of the struggle; for him to give in to the Barnacles, to Mrs Clennam, to his own discouragement and fatigue, would constitute defeat, while to overcome them, to make new commitments, assume new responsibilities, a new family, new life, constitutes victory.

To state this is to raise important questions – what does the struggle represent, how is it won, what is the abstract relation between Clennam's personal situation and the issues with which it becomes involved. In the beginning Clennam is presented as a man completely at a loose end, without purpose towards himself or towards his society. But in London he reveals a sense of mission. Having watched his father's deathbed anxiety, he is preoccupied with a sense of a hidden wrong. 'For heaven's sake let us examine sacredly whether there is any wrong entrusted to us to set right' (Chap. 5), he tells his 'mother', who, shaking her Bible at him, threatens to renounce him if he ever brings up the subject of hidden wrong again. Clennam automatically assumes that the wrong he suspects had to do with money: 'In grasping at money and in driving hard bargains . . . someone may have been grievously deceived, injured, ruined' (Chap. 5). When he offers to set it right he is thinking of cash restitution; he is proposing to give up his property to some unknown person. In fact the guilt which Clennam is searching for exists, and is constituted by what was done to his father, his real mother and himself by Mrs Clennam and his father's uncle, motivated by their religion, their greed, and their hatred of art and joy. Clennam, like Oliver Twist and Esther Summerson, is the child of illicit love. The parallel with Oliver is closer. In both cases the guilt stems from an imposed marriage; the wives forced on Oliver's and Arthur's fathers fulfil remarkably similar roles, even to the suppression of wills. Arthur, like Oliver and Esther, does not know his own identity. Like them, he has been unloved, suppressed, battered, but has kept up his capacity for love. Unlike them, he suspects a mystery, a wrong to redress, and is in a position to take an active part in uncovering the truth. But both his real parents are dead; the only person beside himself whose wrongs can be righted is Little Dorrit, who has been cheated out of a bequest of one thousand guineas. This suppression serves to bring Amy into the Clennam house and prepares for a vital symbolic act at the end of the novel, but it does not represent, in Amy's situation, a wrong toward her comparable to what Clennam and his parents have undergone. Clennam, then, is the surviving sufferer, and his search for the opportunity to make restitution is, without his being conscious of it, a search for his own identity, an assertion of 'will, purpose, hope', and an attempt to make up at forty for the love and joy denied him as a child.

Although it is, in a sense, a coincidence that the wrong he is probing after lies at the roots of the deprivations in his own life, the coincidence reflects a fundamental appropriateness. Clennam's fitness as an emblematic sufferer lies in his having been wronged in his origins and his upbringing. Redeeming oneself by uncovering the guilt in one's origins is a powerful and familiar idea restated from time to time in new terms. It is characteristic of Dickens that he should arrive at the idea from an original direction and without showing any consciousness that what he is doing follows a Christian pattern.*

Clennam, setting out on his search, has no clues and he cannot again ask his mother or Flintwich about the mystery he suspects. His curiosity about Little Dorrit, whom he has seen in a corner of Mrs Clennam's room, gives a new impetus to his investigation of the mystery:

> Influenced by his predominant idea, he even fell into a habit of discussing with himself the possibility of her being in some way associated with it. At last he resolved to watch Little Dorrit and know more of her story. (Chap. 5)

At this point, in Chapters 6 and 7, we are told Little Dorrit's history – of her father's incarceration in the Marshalsea, her birth, her character, and its immunity to the influences which have caused the moral rot of her father, brother, and sister. In Chapter 8 Clennam follows her to the Marshalsea, meets her family, and, having stayed too late, has to spend the night in the Snuggery, where he speculates that perhaps the hidden wrong he seeks is the ruin of the Dorrits, and that his mother compensates for the evil by her kindness to Little Dorrit, and balances Mr Dorrit's imprisonment with her own. This speculation leads to Clennam's attempt to find out the particulars of the action which brought Dorrit to the Marshalsea, which in turn leads to his first brush with the Circumlocution Office. At the Circumlocution Office,

---

* He seems to be doing roughly the same kind of thing, for instance, with baptism in *Our Mutual Friend* (see A. O. J. Cockshut, *The Imagination of Charles Dickens*; London, 1961, pp. 175-9). It is also characteristic that Clennam should (with partial justice) suspect this guilt to be commercial, that a forced marriage should be at the bottom of it, that the guilt of illegitimacy should be fastened not on the parents of the child but upon those who are conceived of as having kept the lovers from marrying.

also on an errand of inquiry and protest, are Mr Meagles and Mr Doyce, whom Clennam meets for the first time.

Dickens thus contrives that the interaction of Clennam's interest in Little Dorrit and his search for his parents' guilt introduce all the relationships with people or institutions which are to be important to him in the book. The trail runs from Amy Dorrit to future partner Doyce, to the Circumlocution Office, of course to the Marshalsea itself; even, in a way, to Mr Meagles and his daughter, Pet, and to Flora Finching. Despite later implications that he has been for a long time Pet Meagles's admirer, Clennam has made no attempt to get in touch with the Meagleses; the meeting at the Circumlocution Office serves as the resumption and quickening of a travelling acquaintanceship which has apparently lapsed. The case as to Flora is even more curious. Twenty years before, Flora and he, presumably infatuated with each other, were separated by their parents. Affery has reminded Clennam of Flora but he has made no effort to see her. On an errand in Amy Dorrit's interest, Clennam finds out from the Plornishes of Bleeding Heart Yard that she has had work from the landlord of the yard, Flora's father, Mr Casby: 'The mention of Mr Casby soon revived, in Clennam's memory, the smouldering embers of curiosity and interest which Mrs Flintwich had fanned on the night of his arrival' (Chap. 13). The wish to help Little Dorrit is his ostensible motive for what is in potential a visit of love: 'With a comfortable impression upon him, and quite an honest one in its way, that he was still patronizing Little Dorrit in doing what had no reference to her, he found himself one afternoon at the corner of Mr Casby's street' (Chap. 13). Thus, through coincidence, and perhaps also through the accession of vigour which having Amy Dorrit as an object of concern seems to work in Clennam, the interest which he feels in her, not consciously involved with desire or love, sets him out on two quests after other women whom he knew before he met her.

The ridiculousness of Flora on the one hand, and, on the other, our sense of shock that Dickens should so cruelly put his old love into his book, ought not to keep us from noticing how important she is in the overall perspective of Clennam's sorrows or how heavy a blow the immediate perception of her qualities is to strike him. Dickens goes to some lengths to explain the effects of this ludicrous disappointment, coming as the culmination of so many other disappointments:

Left to himself again, after the solicitude and compassion of his last adventure, he was naturally in a thoughtful mood. As naturally, he could not walk on thinking for ten minutes, without recalling Flora. She necessarily recalled him to his life, with all its misdirection and little happiness.

When he got to his lodging he sat down before the dying fire, as he had stood at the window of his old room looking out upon the blackened forest of chimneys, and turned his gaze back upon the gloomy vista by which he had come to that stage in his existence. So long, so bare, so blank. No childhood; no youth, except for one remembrance; the one remembrance proved, only that day, to be a piece of folly.

It was a misfortune to him, trifle as it might have been to another. For, while all that was hard and stern in his recollection remained Reality on being proved – was obdurate to the sight and touch, and relaxed nothing of its old indomitable grimness – the one tender recollection of his experience would not bear the same test, and melted away. . . . That he should have missed so much, and at his time of life should look so far about him for any staff to bear him company upon his downward journey and cheer it, was a just regret. He looked at the fire from which the blaze departed, from which the afterglow subsided, in which the ashes turned grey, from which they dropped to dust, and thought, 'How soon I too shall pass through such changes, and be gone!'

To review his life was like descending a green tree in fruit and flower, and seeing all the branches wither and drop off one by one, as he came down towards them.

'From the unhappy suppression of my youngest days, through the rigid and unloving home that followed them, through my departure, my long exile, my return, my mother's welcome, my intercourse with her since, down to the afternoon of this day with poor Flora,' said Arthur Clennam, 'what have I found?'

His door was softly opened, and these spoken words startled him, and came as if they were an answer: —

'Little Dorrit.' (Chap. 13)

The tentative, deprecatory air of the whole episode ('trifle though it may have been to another') and the extreme delicacy about implying that Clennam has in fact thought of taking up with Flora where he left off (elaborate implications that the folly is twenty years old, that it consists in boyhood infatuation rather than in recent anticipation) are presumably to be ascribed to embarrassment. The deprecatory tone, suggesting and perhaps explained by an autobiographical relevance, does not clash with the function of the episode in the plot. Clennam is a subdued and reasonable man with a strong instinct to retreat from his own presumption; his sense of folly and humiliation when Flora stands revealed presumably reinforces this tendency and prepares for his quick retreat in the more important although almost exactly parallel episode of his frustrated courtship of Pet Meagles.

With Pet the pattern is repeated – concern for Little Dorrit leads through coincidence to resumption of an earlier relationship, which is quickly defeated, in one case by the facts of time and character, in the other by these, and by the existence of Henry Gowan; Clennam is thrown back on Little Dorrit, but does not understand himself or her. The effect of these re-enactments is to present a Clennam ever more defeated, ever more desperately in need of redemption which he can only get from Little Dorrit, ever less capable of seizing it.

From Little Dorrit's well-timed announcement of herself, quoted above, and from the visit that follows, we understand that she probably represents Clennam's salvation. We have already been induced to suspect that she is involved in Mrs Clennam's secret, and our suspicions are kept up by Chapter 15 and 29, respectively entitled 'Mrs Flintwich Has Another Dream', and 'Mrs Flintwich Goes on Dreaming'. But essentially nothing happens between them from Chapter 14, describing Little Dorrit's midnight visit, until they come together at the end of the novel. Their characters, neither of which is in itself particularly interesting, do not change; they go on suffering patiently. Amy continues to be excruciatingly dutiful, industrious, and self-effacing; when her father's inheritance is discovered she is tormented for her 'want of proper spirit', and subjected to Mrs General. Arthur, in contrast, is emancipated from his home and background, and the passage quoted above more or less seals up his past sufferings – solidly established, but no longer to be dwelt upon, capable of being transcended in a new life with Little Dorrit. The episode of his love for Pet Meagles, however, follows almost immediately, carrying new cause for suffering. The four chapters which deal specifically with this episode are spaced symmetrically, bracketing the second quarter of the novel: 16, 'Nobody's Weakness'; 17, 'Nobody's Rival'; 26, 'Nobody's State of Mind'; and 27, 'Nobody's Disappearance'. They establish and confirm Clennam's mood in this part of the novel and after. The episode serves in the structure of the novel mainly to knock Clennam down, to make him suffer, to make him lose hope and a sense of his own potentiality. But it has other functions – notably to bring in Gowan, to make the bridge between Arthur's private life and the Circumlocution Office, to connect the novel's attack on the Barnacles and their values to its concern with the idea of unmercenary marriage, marriage for love.

'Nobody' is, of course, Clennam; the name is based on his supposed decision not to fall in love with Pet. Since he has made this decision, such and such incidents do not hurt him, 'and such a state of mind was nobody's, nobody's'. The conceit, which is relentlessly applied, naturally reminds us of *Little Dorrit*'s discarded title, 'Nobody's Fault', and of the political applications suggested by the piece 'Nobody, Somebody, and Everybody', in *Household Words* No. 336 (30 August 1856). These associations, and the pounding reiteration of 'nobody's' may lead us to expect and search for a wider significance in the figure. If it does, the search will be unrewarded; in the context of Clennam's love for Pet, it is an unsuccessful piece of rhetoric, crudely insisting on Clennam's suffering, self-control, and capacity for abnegation.

Clearly the attitudes demanded of us in this episode are not consistent with each other to the extent usual in Dickens; we are expected to see that Clennam ought to marry Little Dorrit and to hope he does so, while at the same time we are expected to sympathize fully with his muffled courtship of Pet, to admire his magnanimity toward his rival, Henry Gowan, and to feel the weight of suffering entailed in his disappointment. There is an apparent shrillness in the emphasis on Clennam's pain, a nagging insistence on how much all this hurts. The obtrusive stress on suffering is probably to be explained in terms of the structural function of this episode, which is, in a sense, the cross-roads of the novel.

If Clennam's role is defined as that of victim and sufferer, then the defeat of his hopes toward Pet Meagles makes a transition from suffering at the hands of Calvinism, Mrs Clennam, and the narrow, grinding, commercial spirit of his early surroundings to suffering at the hands of the Barnacles, of the Circumlocution Office, of Society in Mrs Gowan's and Mrs Merdle's sense. It is essential that Clennam be persecuted by both sides of national tradition – in his background by Roundheads, in his life after his return to England, by Cavaliers. Of the two traditions, the latter, that of the aristocratic jobholders, is in *Little Dorrit* the more important target: it is, of course, the source of the moral rot which infects the Dorrit family. In the first quarter of the novel, however, Dickens has only glanced at it, in Clennam's visit to the Circumlocution Office; now, in Clennam's defeat by Gowan, he moves from one tradition, one target, to the other. Gowan is the bridge between the Barnacles and the personal life of Arthur Clennam. In Gowan and in his mother Dickens presents the analysis which constitutes the most important part of his attack on the Barnacles: their loose sexual ethics, their ruthless and utterly selfish egotism, their laziness, their slippery ability to evade absolute standards of morality, efficiency, truth, their slack, condescending, gentlemanly amateur's attitude towards art — all this evidently not redeemed but aggravated when it goes with charm and cleverness. Outside of Gowan and his affairs Dickens's main charge against the Barnacles is that, through inertia and jobbery, they are misgoverning England. Gowan, of course, has nothing to do with government; that he has not been provided for in the administration constitutes his grievance against his family. Throwing him back on his own resources is for Dickens an opportunity to vary his Crustacean metaphor and undertake, apart from it, a moral anatomy of a member of his ruling class family. It is thus necessary that Gowan's name should not be Barnacle; the name attacks by belittling, and Gowan is evil, not to be belittled, the seducer of Miss Wade, the patron and companion of Blandois, who is represented persistently, if somewhat vaguely, as an incarnation of the Devil. Yet Gowan is indubitably a Barnacle; his wedding, when he marries Pet Meagles for her money, is clearly a characteristically Barnacle affair. Forty Barnacles, including Lord Decimus, come down for the occasion.

Pet is, of course, in love with Gowan. Dickens has come a long way from *Nicholas Nickleby*: this is no Madeline and Gride affair. Gowan is young and attractive. It is nowhere made explicit that he is not fond of Pet, although it becomes quite clear that her being 'the darling only child of a man in very easy circumstances' is a consideration more relevant than whatever he may feel for her. Dickens's unusual subtlety is such that one only comes gradually to understand that this marriage is the result of a radically wicked act of convenience; that it is pre-eminent among the other marriages in the novel – Blandois's, Mrs Clennam's, Mrs Merdle's, Flintwich's, Fanny's – which stand opposite to the marriage of Clennam and Little Dorrit.

Clennam, by the time he meets Gowan and discovers Pet's involvement, has already, it is suggested, 'persuaded himself to set all the earnestness of his nature, all the might of his hope, and all the wealth of his matured character on the cast of his love for Pet' (Chap. 17). Pet's father is his esteemed friend (aside from Little Dorrit and Doyce, his only friend). Given these circumstances, to watch her married to a man whom he must suspect of being a fortune hunter is to sustain helplessly a kind of flagrant but licensed outrage.

Clennam's relation to Pet's marriage is a compound one. He is a jealous rival, a gentleman and good sport, a suddenly middle-aged man whose sense of his own future is almost annihilated by the affair; he is a grave judge of character whose attempts to think well of the bride's choice are frustrated by the weight of evidence, who is constrained by his promise to the bride to hold the uncomfortable position of mediator between her husband and her father. Clennam's position with respect to this marriage illustrates remarkably the problems and complexities involved in the relationship of will and morality in this novel. Dickens speaks of Clennam's 'constant effort not to be betrayed into a new phase of the besetting sin of his experience, the pursuit of selfish objects by low and small means, and to hold instead to some high principle of honour and generosity' (Chap. 26). Clennam wanted to right the old wrong he suspected by giving his property to someone; here his instinct is to give up his hopes, his sense of his own claims, to reject as much as possible the evidence of Gowan's unworthiness, to suppress even the fact of his own involvement – to be 'nobody'. From the narrative tone of the episode there seems no question but that Dickens approves of this self-abnegation. Approval is consistent with the moral analysis implicit in much of the novel. The evil in Mrs Clennam and Miss Wade is largely concentrated in their insistence on having what they want. Their companion Blandois boasts continually of his own abilities, deserts, requirements, power, and status; his conversation is a bare assertion of ego. Morally at the opposite extreme, Little Dorrit's character is one of complete self-abnegation; in a long line of Dickens's heroines who live for others, she carries the principle furthest. As for Arthur, his gentlemanliness is more than a set of manners designed to smooth and dignify social intercourse by sacrificing minor interests and decently muffling major ones – it is a real suppression of self-interest and self-will. Clennam's firmness and perseverance are spent on a series of errands in the service of others – even his vague business career in Doyce and Clennam is represented as a kind of service to his partner – and one becomes oddly uneasy seeing Arthur set forth, again and again, on yet another altruistic task.

We seem to be confronted with a simple analysis of evil as self-will, and with an ideal response to it which retreats from an attack which only menaces oneself, but defends the interests of others. Cavaletto defers to Blandois in the Marseilles jail cell, defers and flees in Chalons, is terrified of being found by Blandois in London, but, in the end, seeks him out and defies him in order to serve Arthur, who is engaged in trying to protect Mrs Clennam's reputation. With the relation of this analysis and this programme to the conflict between Dickens's Christian ethic and his own fierce self-will and occasionally brutal championship of his own interests we cannot be here directly concerned. But as we might expect, *Little Dorrit* is not, in the end, morally uncomplicated; it contains a conflict between the values of self-abnegation, seen as a reaction to and assertion against ruthless self-aggrandizement, and the values of self-confidence, seen as an assertion against the sense of being defeated by life, and against the sense of one's mortality. Clennam is at the same time to himself a man trying to avoid in his own actions the mean and relentless pursuit of personal advantage which has oppressed him all his life, and to us a man whose task is to find 'will, purpose, hope'; to avoid the kind of acquiescence in misery, the passive acceptance of what is thrust upon one finally exemplified in the revealed lives of his real father and mother. One should naturally expect the potential conflict between these two tasks to come into the open in courtship, necessarily an area in which the principle of selflessness cannot operate as elsewhere.

In fact we see signs in Clennam, before Gowan comes on the scene, that he has to some extent developed a will towards the potentialities of his own life — perhaps through the vigour and sense of involvement which his interest in Little Dorrit has brought him. Here are some of his deliberations about himself and Pet; 'He was twice her age. Well! He was young in appearance, young in health and strength, young in heart. A man was certainly not old at forty' (Chap. 16). But when Clennam has seen Pet and Gowan together, this buoyancy completely deserts him, and the principle of selflessness assumes full sway. Nothing Clennam has done has been more virtuous than his conduct under this trial, and none of his previous virtue has been so insisted on:

In the resolution not even to avoid Mr Meagles's house, lest, in the selfish sparing of himself, he should bring any slight distress upon the daughter through making her the cause of an estrangement which he believed the father would regret, there might have been a little merit. In the modest truthfulness of always keeping in view the greater equality of Mr Gowan's years, and the greater attractions of his person and manner, there might have been a little merit. In doing all this and much more, in a perfectly unaffected way and with a manful and composed constancy, while the pain within him (peculiar as his life and history) was very sharp, there might have been some quiet strength of character. (Chap. 26)

The height of merit corresponds with the depth of self-confidence and sense of life; Clennam projects himself into the recurring metaphor of the Thames water flowing quietly past the Meagles's cottage on its way to the sea. He determines that he is too old to be a lover; as he tells Little Dorrit later on:

'I found that the day when any such thing would have been graceful in me, or good in me, or hopeful and happy for me, or any one in connection with me, was gone, and would never shine again.' (Chap. 32)

Clennam's resignation to age and defeat is, of course, wrong, something to be overcome, presumably through the medium of Little Dorrit. It is in keeping with the morality of selflessness that this wrongness should be dramatized more in terms of the damage it does to Amy than to Arthur. Dickens comments immediately on the speech quoted above:

Oh! If he had known, if he had known! If he could have seen the dagger in his hand, and the cruel wounds it struck in the faithful bleeding breast of his little Dorrit! (Chap. 32)

Pet is now out of the way, and only two major obstacles remain between Clennam and Little Dorrit: his conviction that he is past all that, which prevents him from recognizing that he loves her, and her unexpressed but implied sense that his money and position stand between them, that he is above her. Both obstacles are represented as founded on misunderstandings; Dickens makes a conventional sort of drama out of a failure of communications. In doing so he incurs the danger of losing structure and perspective in facile emotional effect – in the pathos of Clennam's mistaken scruples and Little Dorrit's unrecognized love. This is a hazard which the intelligent reader of Dickens is presumably prepared to overcome.

A more important difficulty lies in the effect of the logic behind such drama upon the values Dickens has invoked. Dickens has gone to some lengths to make Clennam's feeling of age and defeat something inflicted upon the man by his whole life's experience, to make it carry a symbolic weight, to involve it with Mrs Clennam and Henry Gowan, and with what they respectively stand for in English society. But now Clennam's exhaustion becomes something which, it is implied, would, if he had known, not only have remained unexpressed, but even have given place to gallantry, awakening love, rejuvenation. On the one hand there is, as we have seen, the heavily reiterated proposition that Clennam really has been terribly battered by his surroundings and there is the implication that what has been done to him is a fair sample of what his society does to decent men. On the other hand there is the suggestion that Clennam's conviction of age and exhaustion is a delusion, that it is bound up in a misunderstanding, that it is to be overcome not even by an act of will, but by simple awareness of another person's love. If this latter suggestion is received in the context of conventional and sentimental dramatic values invited by a good deal of Dickens's description of Little Dorrit and her position, then Arthur's situation is indeed belittled, and his coming together with Little Dorrit dissipates thematic significance and becomes no more than a tired conventional dénouement. The question is whether Dickens's scheme of redeeming Clennam's exhaustion, defeat and depression by giving him Little Dorrit maintains the force and reality, and the representative character, of that defeat and depression.

The crux of the question is the character of Little Dorrit, which is called upon to sustain a tremendous weight, which must counterbalance the largely evil and corrupt economic and social organization of Clennam's world. It seems clear that Amy Dorrit, taken as from one point of view she undoubtedly is — the little Dickens heroine who hurries eagerly about, self-abnegating, modest, humble, shy, mouselike, without independent thoughts and aspirations which she dares articulate — is inadequate to this weight. If the novel, in asking her to bear it, is to be considered successful, then she must be taken as something more than this. Lionel Trilling asserts, for instance, that she is 'the Beatrice of the Comedy . . . the Child of the Parable, the negation of the social will'.* Clearly she ought to be something like these things; yet when we see her and hear her — especially in her relationship to Clennam — when we read her letters from abroad, she seems in her style, in the note she strikes not much more adequate to such a role than, say, Esther Summerson, or even Florence Dombey.

Perhaps one can make a distinction between Little Dorrit isolated or with the man she loves, and Little Dorrit in relationship to the totality of her surroundings; between what is initially postulated about her, and what belongs to the structure of Dickens's plot. With regard to the character, Dickens gives us something familiar which leans heavily upon the values and emotional habits he has appealed to many times before; one thinks of Little Nell, Ruth Pinch, Florence Dombey, Esther Summerson. With regard to circumstances, details which go to make up a symbolic structure, Dickens is much bolder, more rigorous, more successful. This external aspect is, of course, less immediate, more abstract and cerebral; to describe it and insist on it may seem to assert a success in the novel which is more argued

* Lionel Trilling, 'Little Dorrit' in The Dickens Critics, ed. by Ford and Lane.

than felt. Still, when we examine Little Dorrit's multiple relations to her father and the other Dorrits, to Mrs Clennam, to Mrs Merdle, to Blandois, to degradation and poverty, to wealth and high society, it is clear that Dickens has developed these relationships with a complexity and comprehensiveness which go a long way toward supporting her vital position in the novel.

Not only has Dickens worked out the abstract relationships involved in her symbolic role with care and complexity; in a number of passages he gives her character a kind of reflected power by making her a silent but involved witness to brilliantly dramatized aspects of the corruption and wickedness of her surroundings. Dickens's success in representing Mrs Clennam, Mrs Merdle, Mr Dorrit evokes at moments a corresponding vigour in our sense of their moral opposite, Little Dorrit. In the presence of one of these we sometimes become aware of her not so much as a humble, uncomplaining, terribly hardworking little woman who hopelessly adores her blind hero, but as someone gripped by the sadness of an intelligent altruism in ugly and hopeless situations.

The basic metaphor of Amy's relationship to her surroundings is, clearly, of soundness in the midst of rot, purity in the midst of dirt. Dickens presents her soundness to a large extent in terms of economic facts and of attitudes toward money. She earns her keep and more; her family idles and sponges. The contrast extends beyond her family to a society dominated by parasites and confidence tricksters. Little Dorrit's attitudes towards work and money represent the most effective possible curative to a country which admires and follows Barnacles and Merdles, in which the general ambition is for sinecures and unearned riches, in which private relations are dominated by pretensions of status and hopes of gain.

Chapter 20, entitled 'Moving in Society', in which Little Dorrit's sister Fanny takes her to visit Mrs Merdle, offers a good example of the way in which Little Dorrit's relation to her family extends beyond it into the world. Fanny is a snob, despises work, holds fast to the illusion of reduced gentility, and means to use her attractiveness to men to make her fortune. At the great house of the Merdles, Fanny and Mrs Merdle recapitulate for Amy their previous discussions of the question of Fanny and Mr Sparkler, Mrs Merdle's son. Mrs Merdle has promised that if her son married Fanny he 'would be an absolute beggar'; Fanny, furiously asserting her own family pride and position and denying any intentions of marrying Mr Sparkler, has accepted a bracelet and 'a mark or two of my appreciation at my dressmakers' from Mrs Merdle, who is also described as 'putting something in Fanny's hand' as the sisters leave. The scene is one of those previously referred to in which Little Dorrit as a moral force derives a kind of reflected vigour. Although at the centre of the interview, appealed to by both sides, she does not, evidently, say a single word. She observes, disapproves, pities: 'Little Dorrit looked sorry, and glanced at Fanny with a troubled face'. What makes this episode successful – in fact, powerful – is Dickens's presentation of Mrs Merdle and her parrot, which laughs and screams ('Bird, be quiet') and at the close 'suddenly turned himself upside down and trailed himself all over the outside of his golden cage with the aid of his cruel beak and his black tongue'. Standing in mute contrast to images of cold depravity, of life reduced to calculation and display, Little Dorrit can be effective without herself carrying any dramatic initiatives. Out in the street she asks her sister if she likes Mr Sparkler; Fanny responds 'Like him? He is almost an idiot.' Then Little Dorrit says she is sorry Fanny let Mrs Merdle give her anything.

Eventually, in Chapter 51, 'No Just Cause or Impediment why these Two Persons should not be joined together', Fanny marries Mr Sparkler with the approval of all parents concerned. Mr Dorrit is rich and magnificent by this time, a desirable father-in-law for feckless Mr Sparkler, and naturally himself delighted to be allied with the great Merdle; as Dorrit says, 'The name of Merdle is the name of the age' (Chap. 41). Little Dorrit is the only one who tries to stop the marriage. In Chapter 50, 'Taking Advice', she has a long colloquy with her sister, in which Fanny reveals her motives in encouraging Sparkler – these are to avoid being subject to Mrs General, who, she suspects, will soon marry her father, and to achieve a position from which she can torment Mrs Merdle. Little Dorrit protests as vigorously as she can: 'Dear Fanny, let me say first, that I would far rather we worked for a scanty living again, than I would see you rich and married to Mr Sparkler'. What is wrong with the marriage is partly Mr Sparkler's asininity, but mainly Fanny's motives:

'If you loved any one, you would no more be yourself, but you would quite lose and forget yourself in your devotion to him. If you loved him, Fanny' –

Fanny is in her way a shrewd person. She sees her sister's emphasis on the disinterestedness of love as the key to her character ('They say every one has a subject, and I certainly seem to have hit upon yours') and she places her own values and intentions in the context of her background and surroundings:

'Other girls, differently reared and differently circumstanced altogether, might wonder at what I say or may do. Let them. They are driven by their lives and characters, I am driven by mine.'

The marriage of Fanny and Sparkler serves in the plot to tie the Dorrits to the Merdles and to the Circumlocution Office, where a sinecure has been procured for Mr Sparkler. Its function as an illustration of values is, however, even more important. In *Little Dorrit*, as in other novels, Dickens uses mercenary marriage, marriage of convenience, as a central image of the corruption of decent relationships by false values. We have noted how the secret wrong behind Arthur's miserable early life is the commercial marriage his father was forced into, how Gowan's marrying Pet for her money is made to establish the positive wickedness in the values of the class he represents. The issue of honesty and disinterestedness in love stands at the centre of the opposition between Little Dorrit and her society. It is evoked over and over in the contrast she makes with her surroundings; it is even made to come directly into her life, in a curious fashion, with the aspirations of John Chivery.

Chivery's father is the lock-keeper of the Marshalsea, on whom Mr Dorrit, in prison, is dependent for small services. Sensing a coldness in Chivery Senior which he ascribes to his daughter's lack of response to Chivery Junior, Dorrit suggests with parallel anecdotes and increasingly explicit hints, in a crescendo of embarrassment, shame, and self-pity, that Little Dorrit lead the young man on. The scene is calculated with immense skill and subtlety. As in her meeting with Mrs Merdle, Little Dorrit does not say a word. The appeal is made to the strongest motive of her life – to her concern for her father's comfort and dignity. A conflict of values is set up similar to the one presented to Madeline Bray in *Nicholas Nickleby*. Here the issues are externally much less momentous; John is a decent boy, simple and pliable, and all Amy is asked to do is to make him temporarily more cheerful for her father's sake. Of course it is impossible for her to do so. The affair of Chivery is largely calculated to illustrate the complex degradation and shame of Mr Dorrit's character, but it is also notable as the only instance of Little Dorrit's refusing to serve her father. All she can do is to stop his shameful hints by putting her hand to his mouth.

The point is that while Little Dorrit's family and society is preoccupied with deriving money and status from kinship and marriage she insists on working hard and keeping economic life in a separate compartment. Her father furnishes the most powerful and developed example in the book of the confusion to which she opposes herself; social and commercial relations are inextricably involved in his mind.

A long line of Dickens villains, such as Ralph Nickleby, Bray, Sir John Chester, Jonas Chuzzlewit, Pecksniff and Good Mrs Brown, have straightforwardly exploited family relationships for cash. Mr Dorrit, as pernicious in his way as any of these, is not a villain, mainly because he has been so thoroughly corrupted – through the Marshalsea, but essentially by the society of which it is a microcosm — that he is, like an extreme alcoholic, helpless and self-deceptive. As Father of the Marshalsea he lives on cash 'testimonials' to his position; as Little Dorrit's father he accepts an almost total personal sacrifice. In both relations he really thinks he confers status and obligations on his children. In the epoch of his prosperity we are shown how the confusion or transposition of family and money values can apply to spending as well as getting. Little Dorrit is now reproached for trying to do small services for her father; it is much more fitting that these be done by those who are paid. Mr Dorrit hires Mrs General as 'companion, protector, Mentor and friend' to his daughters for four hundred pounds a year. Later he buys from the best jeweller in Paris a 'love gift' and a 'nuptial gift' to bestow on her. This match, one of the most horrible and grotesque in Dickens's novels, is frustrated only by Mr Dorrit's collapse and death.

At the top of society, the Barnacles, like Mr Dorrit, subsist on social status, family connections, and, when convenient or necessary, marriages in which money and status are traded. Dickens makes the same point he made about Dorrit: they think that they have rights to what they can get, and that they confer benefits in getting it. Dorrit, most of the Barnacles, and Mrs Clennam are alike in their ability to conceal fairly successfully from themselves the moral and economic implications of their approach to the problems of making a living and feeding their egos. Mrs Merdle and Gowan understand what they are about, as does Casby, the slum landlord (always referred to as 'Patriarch') who poses as a father to his tenants in order to squeeze them more thoroughly and conveniently,

But the latter group subsists just as much as the former on a confusion of relationships, rationalized in the cases of Gowan and Mrs Merdle by cynical and specious references to the general corruption. The professional classes – 'Bar', 'Bishop', 'Horse Guards' – in their anxious attendance on Merdle, make a similar mutual assimilation of things social and commercial, degrading both categories and betraying their own dignity and integrity. The structure of finance and business, centring around a speculative boom, inside information, the influence of friends and connections, the charismatic power of great names, is a reflection of this pervasive confusion.

Again and again Dickens returns to mercenary or arranged marriage, now enforced as the most effective and important example of the wickedness involved in mixing economic advantages into relations which ought to be based on affection and human need. The marriages of Mrs Clennam, Gowan and Fanny have been referred to. Blandois, the elixir and concentrated principle of evil in the novel, has married a rich widow for her money and pushed her off a cliff when she refused to give him control of it. Affery, forced to marry Flintwich for the convenience of 'the two clever ones', has been pounded by her husband into a condition in which she is not sure when she is awake. Mrs Merdle herself, with her great shining bosom, has made what is in some ways the most blatantly successful mercenary marriage in all of Dickens.

Mrs Merdle, perhaps Little Dorrit's essential opposite number, defines the position of 'Society' towards marriage:

'As to marriage on the part of a man, my dear, Society requires that he should retrieve his fortunes by marriage. Society requires that he should gain by marriage. Society requires that he should found a handsome establishment by marriage. Society does not see, otherwise, what he has to do with marriage. Bird, be quiet!' (Chap. 33)

Mrs Merdle is, of course, given to justifying her own immorality by references to the demands of 'Society'. But in this novel, 'Society requires' is not the same kind of hypocrisy that it would have been in an earlier one. Institutions, conventions, climates of thought have progressively more power over people in Dickens's later novels. The investors in Montague Tigg's Anglo-Bengalee Life Assurance Company are greedy and gullible and thus responsible for their losses; Clennam and Pancks, who succumb to the speculative frenzy organized by Merdle, are sober, cautious, and experienced. In a sense society (with a small s) does require the marriages of Mrs Clennam, Gowan, Fanny, Affery, even Mrs Merdle. The only sense we have of the old freedom in matrimonial-commercial intrigue is with Miss Rugg, who has established a small estate by suing a middle-aged baker for breach of promise of marriage, and who seems out of place — somewhat mechanical — in *Little Dorrit*. Little Dorrit's own marriage to Clennam at the end of the novel thus stands in solitary opposition — like her life and character — to the real values and requirements of her society.

This marriage comes shortly after the other two important elements in the close of the novel — the disclosure of Arthur's parentage and the collapse of the Clennam house. It is involved with these events through several strands of symbolism. Clearly the destruction of the dark prison of Clennam's youth is an appropriate concomitant to the recovery of hope and energy implied in his marriage. The disclosure (although not to him) of the truth about his origins, the discovery that Mrs Clennam is not really his mother, amounts to a backhanded confirmation of trust in life and natural instinct. The discovery that Clennam and Little Dorrit are the surviving members of the secret wrong Clennam suspected in the beginning of the novel reinforces the symbolic significance of their marriage.

When we look closely at the negotiations which lead to the marriage we find that they are largely concerned with money matters, but in the reverse of the usual sense. The point is very strongly made that the destitution of Clennam and Little Dorrit allows them to marry. Clennam's arrival in the Marshalsea exposes him to Young John Chivery, the only person who can tell him that Little Dorrit loves him. That Arthur is ill, in prison, desperately in need of help, brings Little Dorrit to him to offer him all the money she thinks she has. (Her father's total involvement in the Merdle crash has not yet been revealed.) She makes the same point that he has made to Mrs Clennam at the beginning of the novel – that money is no good to her, that the only way she can get any satisfaction out of it is to give it away. It is implicit that Little Dorrit is offering herself with her fortune, and Clennam makes it clear that he loves her, that if he had understood his own mind 'when I was moderately thriving' he would have taken her. But under the circumstances he has to refuse her: 'I am disgraced enough, my Little Dorrit. I must not descend so low as that, and carry you – so dear, so generous, so good – down with me' (Chap. 65).

The next time the subject comes up Little Dorrit knows she has no money. Clennam is getting well, and suggests that it is time for Little Dorrit to go her own way: 'This sacrifice of you must be ended'. But now Little Dorrit has a card to trump his: 'Do you feel quite strong enough to be told what a great fortune I have got?' She teases him: 'You are sure you will not take it?' 'Never.' 'You are quite sure you will not take half of it?' 'Never, dear Little Dorrit.' When she tells him she is penniless his response is to sweep her into his arms:

'I have nothing in the world. I am as poor as when I lived here. . . . O my dearest and best, are you quite sure you will not share my fortune with me now?'

Locked in his arms, held to his heart, with his manly tears upon her own cheek, she drew the slight hand around his neck, and clasped it in its fellow hand.

'Never to part, my dearest Arthur; never any more until the last!' (Chap. 70)

One thing remains to drive the point home: on their wedding morning Little Dorrit gives Clennam a folded paper to burn. The paper is clearly the codicil to Arthur's great-uncle's will entitling Little Dorrit to a thousand guineas, suppressed by Mrs Clennam, recovered by Tattycorum after passing through the hands of Flintwich, his brother Ephraim, Blandois and Miss Wade. Since Flintwich has absconded with much of Mrs Clennam's assets, it might be difficult to restore the money; in any case what is left will come to Arthur when Mrs Clennam dies. But this is irrelevant; Little Dorrit's gesture accomplishes what it intends – a renunciation of money owed by the dark past, an insistence that Clennam and she will enter their marriage clean. Little Dorrit takes the responsibility which Clennam sought in the beginning of the novel – righting the hidden wrong as much as she can by redeeming what remains of his life from hopelessness, and giving up a legacy to do so.

Early in the novel Clennam referred to his parents' religion as 'a gloomy sacrifice . . . offered up as part of a bargain for the security of their possessions' (Chap. 2). In the marriage of Clennam and Little Dorrit an analogous process seems to be working in the opposite direction – a bargain in which possessions are sacrificed in order to secure earthly salvation. Stated in these terms, Clennam's bargain seems more usual, more according to cultural tradition, than the one he accuses his parents of making. Clennam's and Little Dorrit's bargain, however, works in practical rather than psychological terms; it does not amount to paying with one kind of poverty and misery for another kind of affluence and ease. Rather it is an adjustment to the social fact that Dickens's story has enforced – that the way money corrupts is in its divorce from work and its involvement with all the things men do besides work. This is a sufficiently simple and old-fashioned moral, but Dickens is simple and old-fashioned about money, insisting that what makes it good or bad is the way it is gained and spent. The money which gets Clennam out of the Marshalsea and sets him on his feet again is Dan Doyce's; Doyce is, aside from Cavaletto (who, as Blandois's opposite number, carves wooden ornaments for a living), the Bleeding Hearts, and Little Dorrit, the only productive worker in the novel.

CHAPTER V

Great Expectations

IN *Great Expectations* the obsession we have been tracing is worked subtly but with point into Dickens's starkest and tightest plot. The opposition of love and property is more complex than in *Little Dorrit*. In the earlier novel mercenary marriage, as an emblem of general corruption and self-seeking, is symmetrically opposed to the intransigent purity and selfless love of the hero and heroine; in *Great Expectations*, by a subtle paradox, the intention to accept a mercenary marriage becomes involved with the protagonist's romantic self-lacerating devotion to his Intended, and romantic love works in partnership with abject dependence on arbitrary and unearned favours from rich patrons.

Let us look first at the plot structure which establishes the influences by which Pip and Estella are deformed. At the base of this structure is Compeyson, a criminal whose only clearly specified felony has been to defraud a lady whose affections he has engaged. Not only is his wickedness seminal to the important events of the story, it is evidently a fairly important social fact, for Compeyson is finally revealed as a kind of underworld boss: ' "The late Compeyson," said Wemmick, "had by little and little got at the bottom of half the regular business now transacted" '* (Chap. 55). Compeyson is both the

---

* Compeyson may be placed between Blandois and Gowan – simultaneously a desperate criminal and fountainhead of evil and, in birth and breeding, an English

125

'other convict' and the man who broke Miss Havisham's heart by extracting large sums of money from her and failing to appear on their wedding day. As Pip is aware, it would have made more sense for him to have married her.* But Miss Havisham's heart would not have been broken so suddenly; the clocks at Satis House would not have stopped. Compeyson's brutal abandonment of Miss Havisham is less brutal (and less lucrative) than marrying her would have been, but it furnishes a crisis, a dramatic rejection and shattering of illusions. This crisis is almost exactly paralleled by Pip's many years later; the main difference is that Pip does not blame his disappointment only on others.

Miss Havisham and Magwitch both nurse a fierce resentment against Compeyson and what they associate with him: in their different ways they intend Estella and Pip to be the instruments of their revenge upon his memory. Uniting Miss Havisham and Magwitch through Compeyson, as well as through Estella (Magwitch's daughter, Miss Havisham's ward) represents Dickens's traditional method of putting together thematic structures through coincidences in the plot. Although Dickens uses this method in *Great Expectations*

---

* Pip says to Herbert: 'I wonder he didn't marry her and get all the property'. Herbert can only speculate – maybe Compeyson was already married, or maybe her half-brother Arthur insisted on her 'cruel mortification'.

---

gentleman who can manipulate class feeling in his favour. He seems to be, like Blandois and Gowan, an emblematic figure – a ruthless manipulator of others, trading on gentility, prodigal, acquisitive, a passer of bad notes, capable of using the law and the machinery of state in his own interests, clever and powerful – a quintessence of the corrupting forces in his society. It is presumably as such that he stands behind the corruption of Miss Havisham's values (and of Magwitch's) and thus, ultimately, behind the manipulation and distortion of Pip and Estella.

he accomplishes more by implicit comparisons between parallel relationships (Miss Havisham's with Compeyson, Pip's with Estella; Miss Havisham's with her scheming relatives, and with Pip; Pip's with Magwitch, with Joe). In the relation of Miss Havisham and Compeyson Dickens puts together infatuation, romantic disappointment, and cash speculation. He mixes the same elements somewhat differently in Pip's involvement with Estella. Miss Havisham and Pip are infatuated, Compeyson and Estella are calculating, but there is a complication with Pip, who, in his way, calculates too. Pip regards himself as being 'set apart for [Estella] and assigned to her' (Chap. 29) by Miss Havisham. His assumption that Estella is meant for him embarrasses his relations with her — Pip is delicate — but at bottom the assumption pleases and reassures him. When she meets him at the coach office in London Estella seems to hint at their situation, and we are shown that Pip accepts it eagerly:

'I am going to Richmond,' she told me. . . . 'I am to have a carriage, and you are to take me. This is my purse, and you are to pay my charges out of it. Oh, you must take the purse! We have no choice, you and I, but to obey our instructions. We are not free to follow our own devices, you and I.'

As she looked at me in giving me the purse, I hoped there was an inner meaning in her words. (Chap. 33)

As Pip's corruption advances he becomes more and more confused; undoubtedly he believes Estella will come to love him, does not mean to force her affections, and thinks of himself as a disinterested and selfless lover. But the fact is that he intends to take Estella as a gift from Miss

Havisham, part of his expectations, a being who has no choice but to follow her guardian's money. Estella is freer than he thinks; feeling a total inability to respond to love, she marries Bentley Drummle, a man with whom love is out of the question. After she has done it, Jaggers says she married for money, and Jaggers is close to infallible.

Moral corruption spreads in two ways in *Great Expectations*: by overt act – dramatically direct influence – and by seepage from a generally corrupt society. The direct line of infection runs from Compeyson, through Miss Havisham and Magwitch, through Estella, to Pip, who is rotted by his expectations. The expectations are at the centre of the novel, and they are centred on Estella.

Not only Pip, but most of the minor characters who evidence the general corruption of society are given expectations of their own to explain at least partly their moral squalor. Mrs Joe, Pumblechook, the Camillas, Sarah Pocket, the obsequious tradesmen of Pip's town, all make themselves odious or miserable or ridiculous straining after future benefits. An attack on expectations in their broadest sense is in potential an attack on much of the fabric of values and attitudes necessarily erected by a complex commercial and industrial society; it is a sermon on the text, 'Take no heed for the morrow'. In one of its aspects *Great Expectations* is such a sermon and such an attack, with Joe Gargery its exemplar of good.*

---

* Joe's goodness is radically unworldly; he acts according to his standards and is incapable of considering future consequences to himself. His only ambition is moral; he means to do right. He is a great simplifier – 'lies is lies' – and he reduces all dilemmas to moral issues. In a world of Joe Gargerys capital could never be amassed.

Dickens calls attention to the far-ranging implications of his title when he repeatedly invokes the psychology of being in love (miserable but building on a future of bliss), of procrastination, of debt. The point of having Wemmick stage his wedding as if it were something done on the spur of the moment ('Here's Miss Skiffins! Let's have a wedding!') – seems to be to dramatize a salutary avoidance of the psychology of expectation.

'Expectations' – the plural form – carries, of course, a specific sense, and it is this which is primarily meant. When Dickens wrote *Great Expectations* he had been for a long time interested in the moral influence of the prospects of an unearned income upon young men. Young Martin Chuzzlewit is partially warped by such prospects and has to undergo a regeneration through suffering. Walter Gay, who sets out with high hopes to marry his master's daughter, is meant to go bad (Forster's intervention saved him).* Richard Carstone's character deteriorates completely under the influence of his expectations; even Henry Gowan, who, one feels, could hardly in any case have come to good, explains his grossly immoral attitudes toward men and their work by referring to his lifelong expectation that his family would do something for him.

Now Dickens makes the theme central to a novel. The difference between Pip and these earlier characters is not only his centrality, not just that his own progress from innocence to corruption to regeneration by suffering makes up the main substance of the story he tells. Pip's case, in contrast to those of the earlier young gentlemen, is complicated by two aspects – first, his rise breaks

* Forster, II, 341.

through class lines, and second, his love is not opposed
to his ambition, his dependence, and the distortion of his
values, but intertwined with them, necessary to them.
The class aspect Dickens partly muffles; he shows evidence of Pip's new-rich rawness and extravagance, but
the narrative perspective of Pip looking back years afterwards helps him to conceal the immensity of the ascent
from barely literate blacksmith's apprentice to Herbert's
friend and equal (reading 'foreign languages'). The
second aspect – the demonstration of romantic love
working together with social ambition to deteriorate
character – is handled magnificently, and gives the book
much of its power and insight.

It is Estella who first makes Pip understand that 'I
was a common labouring boy; that my hands were
coarse; that my boots were thick; that I had fallen into
a despicable habit of calling knaves Jacks . . .' (Chap. 8).
This is the beginning of his love for her. She shows him
his own poverty and coarseness and the poverty and
coarseness of his background. When Pip, as an apprentice and an adolescent, discusses with Biddy his ambition
and his love for Estella, she asks him 'Do you want to be
a gentleman to spite her or to gain her over?' and he
answers, 'I don't know' (Chap. 17). Before his expectations are revealed to him, Pip's discontent, his growing
patronage of Joe and insensitivity toward Biddy are
explicitly linked to the image of Estella in his mind.
Afterwards, when he is becoming a gentleman, it is
mainly her influence which keeps him from going back to
see Joe – as she says, 'What was fit company for you once
would be quite unfit company for you now' (Chap. 29).
Her influence makes him recoil in horror from Magwitch.

Everything nastily snobbish in Pip, everything which partakes most flagrantly of the effort to deny his origins, is founded on the thought of Estella.

In autobiographical retrospect Pip refuses to analyse or explain his love. He even seems to try to dissociate it from the explanation implicit in the quality of her influence, and of his boyhood dreams of her. He is steadfast in giving Estella no attractions, personal or contingent, besides that of beauty, and in insisting that his love has been an arbitrary infatuation essentially incapable of explanation, to be understood only by reference to the madness of love:

> But though she had taken such strong possession of me, though my fancy and my hope were so set upon her, though her influence on my boyish life and character had been all-powerful, I did not, even that romantic morning, invest her with any attributes save those she possessed. I mention this in this place, of a fixed purpose, because it is the clue by which I am to be followed into my poor labyrinth. According to my experience, the conventional notion of a lover cannot be always true. The unqualified truth is, that when I loved Estella with the love of a man, I loved her simply because I found her irresistible. Once for all; I knew to my sorrow, often and often, if not always, that I loved her against reason, against promise, against peace, against hope, against happiness, against all discouragement that could be. (Chap. 29)

It should be noted that, on the 'romantic morning' referred to, Pip is fully confident that Miss Havisham intends Estella for him and fully confident that she can accomplish her intention. There seems a contradiction between this confidence and the quality of miserable hopelessness Pip claims for his love. Evidently, despite its eloquence, we cannot take Pip's despair seriously; as Julian Moynahan's brilliant essay points out, there is a good deal of moral evasion in Pip's presentation of himself.* Asserting the hopelessness of his love, Pip asserts its disinterestedness, its remoteness from calculation or ambition. But the plain fact is that Pip's love is not, cannot be hopeless. Pip's ambition has fixed itself from childhood on a level too high to be attained by anything within the bounds of rational probability. Once the miracle that makes him a gentleman has been performed – by Miss Havisham, as he thinks – he cannot fail to believe that everything he wants (especially if it is controlled by Miss Havisham) will be given him. It is true that Pip might be confident of Estella's becoming his wife and still despair through the fear that she will never love him. But not only is this psychologically most improbable; there is considerable evidence that he continues to believe, despite her protests, that she can be melted, until the appearance of Magwitch reveals that he and Estella have not been meant for one another.

Pip's ambition is fused with his love into a romantic wish-dream:

She had adopted Estella, she had as good as adopted me, and it could not fail to be her intention to bring us together. She reserved it for me to restore the desolate house, admit the sunshine into the dark rooms, set the clocks a going and the cold hearths a blazing, tear down the cobwebs, destroy the vermin, – in short, do all the shining deeds of the young Knight of romance, and marry the Princess. (Chap. 29)

* Julian Moynahan, 'The Hero's Guilt: The Case of *Great Expectations*', *Essays in Criticism*, X (1960), 60-79.

One recalls that half the kingdom always goes with the hand of the princess in marriage; Pip's confidence in the imminent realization of his dream is largely based on the fact that his half of the kingdom seems already to be secure. There is, however, an important discrepancy between Pip's wish-dream and its fairy-tale model – the young Knight must do 'shining deeds', while Pip's task is only to clean up Satis House, spending his fairy god-mother's money for the purpose. There is no evidence that Pip is lazy or apathetic; we are told that (under Mr Pocket's supervision) he works very hard at becoming a gentleman. But in the social milieu he has made his own there are no shining deeds to accomplish – one has merely to collect one's dividends. Pip's expectations are part of what George Orwell calls 'the strange, empty dream of the eighteenth- and nineteenth-century middle bourgeoisie' which is expressed in phrases like 'the "genteel sufficiency", the "competence", the "gentle-men of independent means" (or "in easy circum-stances")'.* Dickens's assimilation of this dream to the fairy-tale dream, with its proud and glittering princess and its fairy godmother, is a brilliant stroke. The essenti-ally infantile but evidently widely prevalent notion that one is entitled to comfort, ease, and power over the labour of others without doing anything in return is camouflaged by the anxieties and urgencies of romantic love.

Pip's expectations contain a new twist, a new subtlety, in Dickens's presentation of mercenary marriage. Pip loves the girl to distraction; she is what he wants, not

* Orwell, p. 53. Orwell assumes Dickens shares this dream. In this assumption, so far as it concerns evidence from the novels after *Martin Chuzzlewit*, he is quite wrong.

the money which goes with her. In his mind the love comes first, not the money, not the social ambition. But his relation with her (which, it must be remembered, is largely unreal – a set of false assumptions on his part) follows in important respects the pattern of previous forced, mercenary, or arranged relationships in Dickens. The most obvious of these aspects has been mentioned – Estella is to marry Pip at her guardian's behest, without being allowed effective choice in the matter. She is thus to be a kind of victim; her situation is in some respects parallel to that of Edith Granger in *Dombey and Son*. A sensitive young man like Pip in the role of unwillingly accepted husband is something new in Dickens. He is a strange follower of Gride, Pecksniff, Dombey, Heep, and Bounderby, but perhaps at least as cogent a criticism as any of them of the way his society handles love and marriage. In his imagination Pip already has the money that goes with Estella, or the assurance of it; he does not have to marry to be rich. But being rich, becoming a gentleman, denying his origins and his friends, worrying about the opinions of those who despise him, accepting humiliation, indignity and utter passivity – these, to Pip, are all integral with his love for Estella and his intention to marry her. His relation with Estella is not something between two persons, concerning itself with what the two persons are; it is concerned with impersonal things – with class, with status, with habits, occupations, gestures, and language standard in a particular social milieu.

Mercenary marriage in Dickens's novels is always a symbolic activity, representative, broadly, of two drives or activities which concern him – of aggression and violation, and of the intent to live well without working, to

134

rise in society through family connections, influence, flattery, conniving, cadging, rather than by effort and merit. Pip in his own person and conscious intent is innocent of the first drive, although, as Mr Moynahan shows, Orlick and Drummle seem to be his surrogates to carry out appropriate revenge on those (Mrs Joe, Pumblechook, Estella) who have hurt him or annoyed him, and Miss Havisham, who has hurt him most, bursts into flames when he goes back to give her a last long look. The second impetus, which leads ultimately to the confusion of one's love and one's livelihood, Pip has abundantly. Previously, characters in Dickens who wished to accomplish wordly ambitions by marriage were either cynical or petulant or sad – they emphatically did not love those they intended to marry. Disinterestedness and its opposite in the world of Edith Dombey or of Amy and Fanny Dorrit are always fully conscious and clear – altogether out in the open. The nearest thing to an exception to this rule is Henry Gowan, and what he is up to is essentially obvious to everyone but his bride. The insight of *Great Expectations* is that one's interests can control one's emotions in this area as in others. Just as Mrs Joe can work herself into a raging passion by regular stages, so, more subtly, Pip's passion and despair can sanctify his expectations.

By dissociating romantic passion from disinterestedness Dickens seems to take a definite stand on an issue which has been the source of a certain uneasiness in earlier novels. On the one hand Dickens has opposed mercenary marriage to passion, often doomed and hopeless passion – Oliver Twist's father's wife is set against his mother, Sir Leicester against Captain Hawdon, Mrs

Clennam against Arthur's mother; on the other hand he has opposed it to disinterestedness, unselfishness, duty, loyalty – the complex of values represented by Esther Summerson and Amy Dorrit. There is nothing illogical about this; both oppositions make sense. But Little Dorrit, for all her intensity and poignancy, is a figure clearly incapable of reckless passion. Dickens's elevation of the type of heroine which culminates in her seems in definite contradiction to his assertion of the moral value of romantic passion.

Dickens never shows romantic passion – it is always offstage, it is almost always told about as part of the background of the plot. Thus the opposition of mercenary marriage to passion is never dramatized or driven home with anything like the same force as its opposition to disinterestedness and unselfishness. In *Great Expectations* the matter becomes unequivocal; romantic passion is thoroughly discredited by coming together with gross and ungenerous self-delusion in Miss Havisham and Pip, while the example of Biddy, even more than that of Amy Dorrit, furnishes a perspective which reduces passion and romance to egotism and self-indulgence. The pattern of love and duty supplied by Joe and Biddy is fittingly rewarded and completed by a marriage evidently passionless but immensely satisfactory.

Pip dreams of marrying a beautiful lady whom he loves to distraction and living happily ever after on an un-earned income. This is a standard dream; one surmises that it is the achieved ambition of a majority of all the heroes of all the novels written in the eighteenth and nineteenth century. The package of beautiful wife and affluent retirement takes on the dignity of an unquestioningly assumed goal of life; we accept it in somewhat this spirit when it occurs at the end of Dickens's own *Nicholas Nickleby*, *Barnaby Rudge*, and *Martin Chuzzlewit*. In *Great Expectations* the dream corrupts the dreamer, and the closer it seems to come to realization, the more it corrupts him. The important question to be asked is why it is that this dream, involving a goal of life almost universally shared, should be seen as something which corrupts: how does it corrupt? In the case of Pip the evidence for an answer is supplied, and Pip's experience is an indictment of the attitudes and values he shares with his age.

In the first place, Pip's ambition is something anarchic and amoral; it seems to absolve him from human obligations and ties, and to make him a free agent, uninvolved except with what he wants. When Pip's expectations are revealed, the first thing he does is to cut loose from his only real friends, the only people who have loved him and helped him. In the second place, his expectations make him not only idle, but utterly passive in the important affairs of his life. It is true that Pip rises through class lines, but to equate him (as a modern critic has done)* with young men like Julien Sorel who drive upward on nerve and talent is quite misleading. The word 'expectations' is explicit and appropriate; in the circle of gentility where Pip has been placed one waits for one's destiny and accepts it. Money is what counts, but making money is vulgar; a genteel young man must

* A. Robert Stange, 'Expectations Well Lost – Dickens's Fable for his Time', *The Dickens Critics*, ed. Ford and Lane, pp. 295-9.

have wealth to begin with or acquire it passively. This is one reason for the recurrent fables in eighteenth- and nineteenth-century fiction of discovered identities and suppressed wills – one gets the inheritance, but actually one had it all along.*

Passivity like Pip's is undignified and enervating. The life Pip leads after his expectations have been revealed is largely foolish, boring and unproductive.† In Pip's circumstances one is not merely passive – one fawns and cringes before one's potential benefactors. Pip is ostensibly set apart from the revolting crew of Miss Havisham's relatives, but his situation is quite similar to theirs – both he and they expect or hope to make their fortunes by pleasing Miss Havisham. Miss Havisham's wealth and Pip's belief that she is his benefactress change her, in his eyes, from a fantastic eccentric maniacally pursuing a foolish obsession in dark squalor, to a fairy godmother. It should be remembered that Miss Havisham has been wearing her wedding dress continuously for at least twenty years, that she carries one slipper in her hand, excludes all daylight, and eats only at night when no one can see her. The most moral course to take with such a being (if one cannot effectively intervene) is that of Mr Pocket, who, having warned her and

* A thorough and illuminating discussion of the relation between property and the hero's passivity – specifically in terms of the novels of Scott – occurs in Alexander Welsh's *The Hero of the Waverley Novels* (New Haven, 1963).

† It is true that Pip acquired an education, and even if this education is taken as no more than the polish necessary to pass as a gentleman – a set of tags and common references – acquiring it would, in reality, have made his life busy, difficult, and challenging indeed. But we cannot take Pip's learning seriously as the hard won accomplishment of a blacksmith's apprentice. Quite arbitrarily we are shown Pip reading to Magwitch ('foreign language, dear boy'); he is a young gentleman now, and young gentlemen read books in foreign languages.

advised her plainly and as forcibly as possible, now holds himself aloof. Pip's relation to Miss Havisham dramatizes the power of the dream of an unearned income to distort clear vision, and thus to destroy dignity, moral courage, and rational judgment.

When Magwitch comes and reveals himself the dream collapses: 'All the truth of my position came flashing on me; and its disappointments, dangers, disgraces, consequences of all kinds, rushed in in such a multitude that I was borne down by them and had to struggle for every breath I drew' (Chap. 39). Pip reacts to two discoveries – that of who his patron is, and who he isn't. His reactions to these two facts become confused with each other and produce a tangle of ambiguities. As soon as he knows that his money has come from Magwitch, Pip's mixture of embarrassment and kindliness toward the convict gives way to extreme revulsion: 'The abhorrence in which I held the man, the dread I had of him, the repugnance with which I shrank from him, could not have been exceeded if he had been some terrible beast' (Chap. 39). Pip's horror is not openly explained, although there is the suggestion that it is founded on the connection established between criminality and his own fortune: 'He laid his hand on my shoulder, I shuddered at the thought that for anything I knew, his hand might be stained with blood' (Chap. 39). Much is made of the taint of Magwitch's money — Pip cannot take any more of it; he must go into debt and sell his jewelry, the situation is terribly embarrassing to Pip's sense of his class position. Pip cannot think that his money is the fruit of crime, but the idea of being an Australian convict's 'bought-up London gentleman'

(Magwitch's phrase) is uncomfortable – quite different from, say, deriving one's income from shares in Australian lands and mines. The class humiliation is not openly faced – Pip tries to work it into a moral reaction to criminality; to put the stamp of morality on his emotions he invokes the figure of Joe:

> But sharpest and deepest pain of all – it was for the convict, guilty of I knew not what crimes, and likely to be taken out of these rooms where I sat thinking, and hanged at the Old Bailey door, that I had deserted Joe. (Chap. 39)

That Pip's money comes from Magwitch is a discovery fertile in class ironies and in reflections on the source of unearned incomes, but to Pip it is less important than its corollary – that the money has not come from Miss Havisham:

> Miss Havisham's intentions toward me, all a mere dream; Estella not designed for me; I only suffered in Satis House as a convenience, a sting for the greedy relations, a model with a mechanical heart to practice on when no other practice was at hand; those were the first smarts I had. (Chap. 34)

There is evidence that Pip even clings momentarily to the hope that part of his money may have come, after all, from Miss Havisham. ('Was there no one else,' I asked. 'No,' said he, with a glance of surprise, 'who else should there be?')

Pip's situation is strikingly parallel to Miss Havisham's on her wedding morning. He has merely been used; Estella has not been intended for him; his world is in ruins. But Estella has never pretended to love him, has never encouraged him, has told him, when he complained of her never giving him looks and smiles like those she gives Bentley Drummle, that she only smiled to deceive and entrap. She has asked him, 'will you never take warning?' (Chap. 38); she has inquired if he wants to be deceived and entrapped too. The shock cannot be that of suddenly realizing that Estella does not love him; he never thought she did, but only hoped weakly that, adjusting herself to the accomplished fact of her bestowal on him, she might come to do so. What plunges Pip into despair and makes him consider the decent equivalent of suicide (enlisting for India as a private soldier) is the understanding that he has never been meant by Estella's guardian to have Estella, that the connection he has made between Estella and his own fortune and gentility is a false one. This understanding completely undermines his position and makes him wish he had never left the forge. The point is not that he now realizes that he has deserted Joe for a convict (with the startling implication that it would have been all right to desert him for a half-crazed rich old maid); rather it is that he has never really understood until now the fact of his desertion of Joe or of his metamorphosis into a shallow snob; he has never suspected the loss of his own dignity. As soon as his dream is shattered he sees immediately what he could not see before, when he thought that what he was doing and what he had become was done for Estella. As long as Pip thinks Estella is meant for him, her image in his mind obscures decency and self-knowledge. The arrival of Magwitch does not, however, cure Pip immediately of his habit of self-delusion.

Assuming that Pip still wants Estella, he is still as

able to acquire her as he ever was, as far as his own qualities and abilities are concerned. With a crudity evidently agonizing to Pip, Magwitch suggests a campaign to gain Pip's heart's desire:

> 'There's bright eyes somewheres – eh? Isn't there bright eyes somewheres, wot you love the thoughts on?'
> O Estella, Estella!
> 'They shall be yourn, dear boy, if money can buy 'em. Not that a gentleman like you, so well set up as you, can't win 'em off his own game; but money shall back you!' (Chap. 39)

The thought of renewing the pursuit under new auspices is evidently abhorrent. When one asks why, one finds that the red herring of tainted money has been drawn across the track; having Estella on Magwitch's money instead of Miss Havisham's would profane her. If it were Estella as a person whom Pip loved, and not what she represents in the structure of his expectations, Magwitch's money could not profane her in being spent by or for her. Dickens makes this point (among others) with one of his plot coincidences – Magwitch is Estella's father. Pip's horror of the convict's money is based on his delusions – it is false pride and empty snobbery.*

When Pip next goes to Satis House he makes a declaration of love to Estella, but one predicated on the assumption that nothing will come of it. He explains his previous silence as delicacy:

> 'I should have said this sooner, but for my long mistake. It induced me to hope that Miss Havisham meant us for one another.

* This is a complex matter. It is undoubtedly right that Pip should not be enriched, after all, by Magwitch; that he should have to work for his living. But the idea that the convict's money is dirty is gone at the end, and an effort is made to save it for Pip.

While I thought you could not help yourself, as it were, I refrained from saying it. But I must say it now.'

Preserving her unmoved countenance, and with her fingers
still going, Estella shook her head.

'I know,' said I, in answer to that action, – 'I know. I have no
hope that I shall ever call you mine, Estella. I am ignorant what
may become of me very soon, how poor I may be, or where I may
go. Still, I love you. I have loved you ever since I first saw you in
this house.' (Chap. 44)

This speech is not altogether honest. Pip has actually
declared his love for Estella many times, in many ways.
As he says on this very occasion, she already knows he
loves her; it has been perfectly understood between
them for a long time. If he has refrained from pushing his
suit importunately it has been because she has given him
no encouragement, and because of the passivity of his
romantic dream. He has been waiting for Miss Havisham to overcome Estella's stubborn coldness, to arrange
matters, and to set a date. Now he has no hope; why
not? Pip's speech implies that the reason is that he is uncertain of his future and will soon be poor. But Pip is a
rich man if he is willing to be one. Unwillingness must
come either from his making a moral distinction between
Miss Havisham's money and Magwitch's or from a
whole new perspective which he has gained from the
shattering of his delusion, a perspective which keeps
him from wanting to have his fortune made by anyone.
Pip's reasons for expecting to be poor can thus be good
or bad; they can belong either to the corrupt phase
from which he is beginning to emerge or to his regeneration. Dickens leaves the matter ambiguous; ambiguity

is appropriate to the confusion of Pip's moral crisis and transition.

A second possible reason for the hopelessness of Pip's love is that he knows Estella does not love him. This knowledge, which he has always had, never made him hopeless before. But under the shock that he has sustained, his values and his perception are improving; he may really see and understand for the first time the importance of Estella's inability to love.

Whatever other reasons are stated or suggested, the essential reason why Pip's love is hopeless is that it is now a fragment of a shattered thing. It has always been integral to his expectations; it is not viable apart from them. Although it claims to be personal, individual, romantic, intense, it depends for its life upon patronage and outside arrangement – upon the thought of money and authority from Miss Havisham.

Before he leaves Satis House Pip makes another eloquent speech, one which shows the extent to which Estella has been not herself, but a symbol and an illusion to him:

'You are part of my existence, part of myself. You have been in every line I have ever read, since I first came here, the rough common boy whose poor heart you wounded even then. You have been in every prospect I have ever seen since – on the river, on the sails of the ships, on the marshes, in the clouds, in the light, in the darkness, in the wind, in the woods, in the sea, in the streets. You have been the embodiment of every graceful fancy that my mind has ever become acquainted with. The stones of which the strongest London buildings are made are not more real, or more impossible to be displaced by your hands, than your presence and influence have been to me, there and everywhere, and will be. Estella, to the last hour of my life, you cannot choose but remain part of my character, part of the little good in me, part of the evil. But in this separation I associate you only with the good, and I will faithfully hold you to that always, for you must have done me far more good than harm, let me feel now what sharp distress I may. Oh, God bless you, God forgive you!' (Chap. 44)

Estella's reaction to this is – as well it might be – 'incredulous wonder', but the speech melts Miss Havisham who, at its close, 'seemed all resolved into a ghastly stare of pity and remorse'. Dickens is clearly moved, and seems himself to be involved in the self-pity and self-deception of the speech, in its spurious generosity, its egotism, its self-conscious poetic sensibility, its gratuitous piety. Estella did not ask Pip to construct his life around her; she is not responsible for his fancies, nor even for the coldness of her own disposition. It is an indication of Dickens's immense strength and complexity that he can sweep himself and his audience away on such a current of self-pity and wounded egotism, involve himself and us in its evasions and distortions, and yet give us all the evidence to see it, on reflection, exactly for what it is.

God is adjured to forgive Estella, but she is to be adequately punished all the same by marrying Bentley Drummle, the upper-class equivalent of Orlick. It is difficult to explain her marriage. Jaggers says she married for money (which she doesn't need; she has Miss Havisham's). Clearly Drummle's wealth is a reason for marrying him, but she could undoubtedly have married for money someone less likely to beat her. Pip thinks that Miss Havisham is forcing the marriage, but Pip has always overestimated Miss Havisham's ability to guide her ward's choice in these matters, and in fact Miss Havisham is trying to delay the fatal step. Estella implies that she has chosen Drummle because she is tired of her present way of life and would rather inflict her coldness upon a brute than a decent man. Whatever difficulties there are in accepting this (the exquisite moral sensibility it demands from Estella, the willingness of a physically and emotionally cold woman to marry the man least likely to respect her coldness), it seems the most reasonable explanation within the dramatic structure of the novel.

But there are two good reasons for having her marry Drummle operating outside this structure. Drummle has two aspects. As sinister amphibian creeping along under the riverbank after Startop and Pip, as thick-tongued sub-human lout whose only resource in a dispute is to violence, he seems a figure expressly invented to punish a fine cruel lady. As the rich scion of a fine old family, a person immensely appreciated by the idiotic genealogist Mrs Matthew Pocket, he represents the kind of man society may be expected to consider a good match. Thus Dickens constructs simultaneously a purgatory for Estella (it is remarkable with what grim satisfaction Jaggers is made to discuss the question of whether Drummle will 'beat or cringe') and a conventional mercenary marriage – a reality to set up against Pip's glittering illusion.

With Pip's expectations altogether shattered and with Estella punished, Dickens has one major task and one minor one: he has to show how his hero understands his lesson and what he does with it, and he has to dispose of

Magwitch. The problem of Magwitch Dickens handles consummately. It is clearly necessary for him to die, but to die happy; this is accomplished without any sense of strain or manipulation. Magwitch is too old and too simple to be subjected to any lessons on the moral complexities involved in buying up London gentlemen; he has meant well. Pip is loyal and loving, fostering his illusions, making him think that his money is safe and his gentleman rich. At the last, Pip gives Magwitch a final illusion to die on. Estella, he says, 'lived and found powerful friends. She is living now. She is a lady, and very beautiful. And I love her.' Magwitch dies in the sweet faith that his daughter (by this time Mrs Bentley Drummle) will be married to his foster son.

It is all right for Magwitch to have this faith, but not for the rest of us. The patched-on second ending is a great mistake, false in substance and in tone; the original ending is incomparably better. It is quite true that Pip and Estella, meeting after years, have been purged and regenerated by suffering, and that, since they are radically changed persons, there is nothing logically objectionable in Pip's seeing 'no shadow of another parting' (Chap. 59). But their marriage is pointless, purely a sentimental gesture. What was between them was all on Pip's side and was bound up with Pip's now shattered expectations. Even an ambiguous and muted coming together of Pip and Estella makes one of two false suggestions – that something has survived of the complex of Pip's foolish dreams, or that Estella is separable in his mind from this complex.

Furthermore it contradicts the lesson Pip has learned – that, while one must not fix oneself, like Miss Havisham, in sterile brooding over one's hurts, one cannot go back and start again. After Pip's crisis and delirium, when Joe is nursing him, Pip tries to be a child with Joe again: 'I was slow to gain strength, but I did slowly and surely become less weak, and Joe stayed with me, and I fancied I was little Pip again'. Trying to be little Pip, to start again, Pip has attempted to follow through on his realization that Biddy was the person he ought to have married, not only to secure her virtues for his improvement, peace, and comfort, but because, unlike Estella, she offers the potentiality of real love. But Pip has found that he has forfeited his right to her.

Class necessarily figures in the situation; Dickens's contemporary readers presumably felt more strongly than we do the consideration that a class barrier now separates Pip and Biddy, that London life has left him closer to Estella than to his childhood friend. This consideration is a mistake, and an important one; it is encouraged by the second ending. Class differences are real, but not so real to Dickens as to others. To Dickens, whose grandfather and grandmother were domestic servants, what supports genuine class distinctions is education alone. Pip is now educated, but Biddy is a schoolmistress. In Dickens's terms there is more of a class barrier between Joe and Biddy than between Pip and Biddy. But just as Bentley Drummle is Estella's punishment, so Biddy is Joe's reward; he deserves her. Pip deserves no more than the chance he earned with his one act of disinterested generosity when he was rich — the chance to work for his keep in kindly surroundings.

CHAPTER VI

Our Mutual Friend

THE relation between marriage, money, and the values of 'Society' is the explicit subject of Dickens's last completed novel. The main plot of *Our Mutual Friend* concerns a mercenary marriage set up by the will of an immensely rich dust collector – a marriage which eventually takes place when changes in their situations and characters have allowed the parties to it to love each other disinterestedly; the subplot is about an indolent, purposeless young gentleman morally redeemed by the love of a working girl, whom he marries in defiance of the not quite united voice of 'Society'.*

Our Mutual Friend is a return to the 'broad canvas' of twenty monthly numbers, not only twice as long but much looser than either of the two previous novels (which came out in weekly instalments in *All the Year Round*). Dickens seems to have made his first approaches to it not in terms of its plot structure but of isolated characters and situations. According to Forster, the 'three leading notions on which he founded the story' were, first, of the bodies in the Thames and the men who fished them out and robbed them, second, of ' "a man, young, and perhaps eccentric, feigning to be dead, and *being dead* for all intents and purposes external to him-

---

* Dickens entitles his last chapter, in which the circle of the Veneerings judge Wrayburn's marriage 'The Voice of Society'.

self" ', and third, of ' "a poor imposter of a man marrying a woman for her money, she marrying *him* for *his* money; after marriage both finding out their mistake, and entering into a league and covenant against folks in general": with whom he had proposed to connect some Perfectly New People'.* Evidently the covenanted couple (who become the Lammles) were intended to play a more important part than they do in establishing the tone of the Veneering's circle. In the event, the moral and intellectual level of 'Society' is established not nearly as much by the Lammles as by Podsnap and Lady Tippins. But the plan of having a couple marry each other for money is adapted, in far more complex, less conventional guise, to the situation of the young man who pretends to be dead.

This young man is John Harmon, alias Rokesmith, a character with some similarities to Arthur Clennam. Harmon's father, the rich dust collector, of all bad fathers in Dickens seems to have been the worst. We are told that his 'moral being' . . . 'derived its highest gratification from anathematising his nearest relations and turning them out of doors' (Bk. 1, Chap. 2). This he has done to his wife, son, and daughter; the daughter on grounds of her unwillingness to marry the man of her father's choice (even endowed with a marriage portion of 'I don't know how much Dust, but something immense') the son because he has tried to intercede for his sister.

At the beginning of the novel Old Harmon has been dead about a year, leaving a will which settles one of his dust mounds on Mr Boffin, his illiterate and goodhearted foreman, and the rest of the property on his son,

* Forster, III, 371-72.

provided that young John marries Bella Wilfer, the daughter of a poor clerk; if the marriage fails to take place, everything goes to Boffin. Old Harmon seems to have selected Bella for her disposition – he had seen her as a small child stamping her foot, screaming and beating her father with her little bonnet.

In the scope of its intent and of its symbolic association, the marriage Old Harmon intends for his son goes beyond any previous mercenary marriage in Dickens. The marriage is to be forced, but forced by irresistible self-interest, by a grip stronger than that of living will, irrevocable, from beyond the grave, supported by the laws of England. The marriage is to be grossly mercenary; both parties are to marry for money; both are to be fully aware of what they are doing. It is, if possible, to be unhappy – Old Harmon tries to select a termagant as his son's wife. The property for which John and Bella are to marry is literally dust – a word expressing every form of London's waste, including human faeces. As a final twist, Old Harmon has scattered more recent wills around the property – the latest one leaving everything to Boffin. He presumably expects these wills to take the inheritance away from his son after his son has married for it, and to involve all parties in the endless litigation of another Jarndyce and Jarndyce.

Where in *Great Expectations* Pip of his own initiative involves Estella with his hopes of gentility and unearned wealth, and puts together blindly and fortuitously the structure of expectations and romantic infatuation which corrupts him, here everything except the final twist – the hidden wills of later date – is clear, deliberate, out in the open. There is an open challenge to John Harmon and

Bella to prostitute themselves. Curiously, both seem willing to do so, although both are troubled by the necessity. Bella, as we learn afterward, accepts the idea that a stranger is to be her husband and that she is to be rich. John Harmon, located by advertisement, makes a forced sale of his little farm at the Cape of Good Hope and takes ship for London. But his uneasiness is strong enough to make him form vague plans to see something of Bella without her knowing who he is.

The question arises, how can Dickens allow a young man unequivocally his hero, a man whose conduct is clearly meant at every step to be approved, even to hesitate in such a matter? Does not allowing such a young man to sell his farm, forsake his independent livelihood, and come to London with whatever hesitations and reservations to claim an inheritance bound by such conditions, show an appalling lack of moral sensitivity — a lack in precisely that area where Dickens has in book after book shown himself most sensitive? Richard Carstone's hopes to inherit wasted his body and mind, Lady Dedlock's marriage destroyed her, Little Dorrit burned her thousand-pound codicil, Magwitch's money went to the Crown, and Pip could take nothing from Miss Havisham. Has Dickens finally accepted the idea that it is impossible for a sane man to turn down a hundred thousand pounds; or does he allow himself, in his fatigue, to adopt the same romantic confusions he punished in Pip?

The answer to these questions is contained in the nature of Dickens's fable and centred in the figure of Bella Wilfer. Bella might turn out to be an ideal mate, a person whom Harmon would love under any circum-

stances, and who would love Harmon, rich or poor.
This, of course, is Harmon's romantic hope in coming to
London, and it bears some similarity to Pip's early hopes
for himself and Estella. This hope fulfilled, the way will
be clear for the working out of a familiar romantic drama:
once circumstances have been contrived through which
Bella and Harmon can prove the purity of their love,
they can marry. The money will come only as an extra
dividend to their joy, a reward for their goodness and lack
of greed.

Dickens's fable has some similarities to the conventional one but its differences are crucial. In the first place,
Bella is no Amy Dorrit. As Harmon himself reflects
when he comes to know her, she is 'so insolent, so trivial,
so capricious, so mercenary, so careless, so hard to
touch, so hard to turn' (Bk. I, Chap. 16) – in fact a good
deal like Estella. But unlike Estella she has a passionate nature; she is selfish and thoughtless and vain, but
impulsive, quick, responsive, potentially sensitive, and
affectionate. In her Dickens undertakes for the first
time to show a capricious young woman with real
depth, and to show such a character improving, coming
into her potentialities. The often-made speculation on a
possible relation between Bella and Ellen Ternan is supported by the crucial importance which Bella's reformation has in this book. If she can be reformed, then 'the
fate which seemed to have fallen upon my father's riches
– the fate that they should lead to nothing but evil' (Bk.
II, Chap. 13) will be defeated and reversed. Old Harmon's malevolence will be frustrated and the corruption and misery he meant to work turned to their opposites.

Bella's character is the most important of three factors which distinguish Dickens's fable from the ordinary one. In the ordinary fable the hero often disguises himself or pretends to be poor. Harmon does both, but his disguise is radical; he dies and becomes a new person. And finally, Harmon not only pretends to be poor; he actually is poor – he has no legal rights to any of his father's dust under any circumstances. Old Harmon's extra twist, his last will, has given everything to Boffin. The seemingly pointless plotting and counter-plotting which goes on around the ridiculous Silas Wegg acquires point when one sees that in making Boffin probate this last will it emphasizes that John's and Bella's marriage cannot possibly be mercenary; John knows before he marries her that the will alloting her to him is not legal, and Bella thinks she is marrying a man who has no money.

Harmon's disguise is necessary to Bella's reform. As Harmon later sees, 'her faults have been intensified by her place in my father's will' (Bk. ii, Chap. 13). The only way for Bella to lose her corrupting expectations without being confronted and discarded by Harmon is for him to die. But he does not assume his disguise deliberately; it is thrust upon him. Dickens arranges circumstances through which, without intention, guilt, or violence on Harmon's part, a body, considerably decayed, wearing his clothes with his papers in the pockets, is recovered from the Thames and proclaimed as his. Harmon, who has himself been drugged and nearly drowned, and who is slowly recovering, has not yet told anyone his name. He seizes the chance to assume a new identity, and becomes first Julius Handford and then John Rokesmith.

As Rokesmith he takes lodging in Bella's house and gets employment as Boffin's secretary. The Boffins, who last saw him at the age of seven, do not recognize him for some time.

Dickens's germinal idea of a young man 'feigning to be dead' is thus worked into the mechanics of his plot. The connection between this idea and the defeat of Old Harmon's designs against his posterity is, however, more than mechanical. John Harmon comes back to England uneasy, divided, suspicious of himself:

'When I came back to England, attracted to the country with which I had none but most miserable associations, by the accounts of my fine inheritance that found me abroad, I came back, shrinking from my father's money, shrinking from my father's memory, mistrustful of being forced on a mercenary wife, mistrustful of my father's intention in thrusting that marriage on me, mistrustful that I was already growing avaricious, mistrustful that I was slackening in gratitude to the two dear, noble, honest friends [the Boffins] who had made the only sunlight in my childish life or that of my heart-broken sister. I came back, timid, divided in my mind, afraid of myself and everybody here, knowing of nothing but wretchedness that my father's wealth had ever brought about.' (Bk. ii, Chap. 13)

Like Arthur Clennam, Harmon needs to break away from his past and his origins; he needs a new identity, a name which is not his father's, not only to prove Bella but for his soul's good. Like Wrayburn later on, he comes out of the river a different man. The analogy to baptism has often been noticed*; what I mean to stress

* A particularly strong and interesting analysis of the symbolism of the river is to be found in A. O. J. Cockshut, *The Imagination of Charles Dickens* (London, 1961), pp. 175-9.

is not the connection between Harmon's new identity and the pervasive symbolism of the river, but the necessity of this new identity to his defeating his father's plot against him. As Harmon he was being helplessly if uneasily driven by his father's will towards a wretched mercenary marriage; as Rokesmith he has not only a breathing space and the chance to look Bella over incognito, but the independence and confidence to decide he will not marry her for money. Ultimately, as Rokesmith, he acquires sufficient distance from his father and liberty from the dread of being forced by his father which has haunted his life, to love disinterestedly the girl his father has chosen for him and to be a person who can compel her love and bring out her better qualities. This may seem like coming the long way round to do his father's will, but it is not. It is a mistake to assume that Dickens is psychologically not sophisticated enough to be aware that the power to taint good things by forcing them on others is one of the ugliest aspects of arbitrary power. By becoming John Rokesmith, John Harmon escapes his father's power to taint as well as his power to coerce.

In *Our Mutual Friend* Dickens's obsession with inadequate or evil parents is related more strikingly to his obsession with mercenary marriage than ever before in his novels. The basic connection is plain: mercenary or arranged marriage compellingly exemplifies the power of elders over the lives and choices of their children, exerted either directly or through the power to warp their values and development. Before *Our Mutual Friend* this connection is shown most tellingly in the novels – especially *Little Dorrit* – in which mercenary marriage is contrasted not with romantic passion, but with marriages meant to fulfil the needs for companionship and comfort of quiet, steady young men and women. Fathers and mothers in Dickens almost always work against their children's marrying to suit their own true needs, and often they force or promote mercenary marriages. On the other hand, the surrogate fathers who populate Dickens so thickly from Pickwick to Boffin are always for liberty in love and marriage. The important characteristics of these surrogates – Pickwick, the Cheerybles, Captain Cuttle, Jarndyce, Joe Gargery, Boffin – are that they make no claims for themselves and exert no authority. Bella Wilfer's real father, one of the few good ones in Dickens, qualifies for his daughter's trust and affection by his resemblance to the surrogates in these respects:

'I don't mind telling *you*, because we have always been favourites of each other's, and because you are not like a pa, but more like a sort of younger brother with a dear venerable chubbiness on him. And besides,' added Bella, laughing, as she pointed a rallying finger at his face, 'because I have got you in my power.'* (Bk. II, Chap. 8)

Bella's father is shocked by her admission of the growing necessity of riches to her, and by her schemes to marry money; he later enters eagerly and with relief into Bella's plan to marry the penniless secretary John Rokesmith. His complicity must at all costs be concealed from the majestic Mrs Wilfer, the power in the house-

---

* A real father to set against Rumty Wilfer is Old Bill Barley, the retired purser in *Great Expectations* who roars and thumps on the floor of the room over Magwitch's retreat. Old Bill's death is awaited with the most lively impatience by his daughter and her suitor, Herbert Pocket, who are imprisoned by his demands, and who want to marry and be free.

hold, who bears most of the responsibility for the false values Bella must overcome in herself.

What Dickens evidently dislikes and fears in the relation between parents and children is the fact of power, the near-absolute authority of one person over another's life; he cannot imagine a good relationship under such a condition. This power is basically economic; the father's ultimate threat is to withdraw his support, to disinherit his child. He is particularly apt to do this (as Mr Harmon does with his daughter) when his child marries without his consent or opposes his plans for its marriage. Personal and selfish interests, like those of Mr Bray and Sir John Chester, sometimes motivate a father when he forces his child's choice in marriage, but often he does so because he shares the corrupt values of society and is incapable of understanding or acting upon the child's true interests. The Dickens surrogate father, on the other hand, is an odd character who cannot possibly be aligned or identified with the dominant values or habitual attitudes of society. Even when he is rich his values are unmercenary and it is hard to see how he could have made any money. He sometimes urges his simple and unwordly standards on his foster child, but always carefully avoids using his money to coerce.

Old Harmon, an extreme eccentric himself, can be identified with the presiding spirit of society through the symbolism of his accumulated mounds of refuse (much as Krock is identified with the Lord Chancellor through his rag and bottle shop) and perhaps through the name his establishment has been given, 'Harmony Jail'. The old man's malignity is not explained and seems motiveless, but the power he exerts in his attempt to crush the son who has fled him is one unique to fathers, the main weapon in a father's armoury. His son escapes him by taking a new name and by denying his own origin. John Harmon achieves his triumph and ultimately gets the money on his own terms through Boffin, the surrogate father, who has no authority and no obligations, but gives out of love and of his own free will. John tells Silas Wegg near the end of the novel:

'You supposed me, just now, to be the possessor of my father's property, – so I am. But through any act of my father's, or by any right I have? No! Through the munificence of Mr Boffin . . . I owe everything I possess solely to the disinterestedness, upright-ness, tenderness, goodness (there are no words to satisfy me) of Mr and Mrs Boffin.' (Bk. IV, Chap. 14)

Such eulogy is beyond the reach of real parents, who at the best can only fulfil their obligations (and seldom, in Dickens, achieve even this).* Boffin not only approves of John's disinterested marriage; he and Mrs Boffin make it possible by contributing vitally to Bella's reform, and by putting John in heart when he is discouraged and about to give her up. As soon as the Boffins have recog-nized John and understand that he is in love with Bella, Boffin reassures him about her character:

'She may be a leetle spoilt, and nat'rally spoilt,' he says, 'by cir-cumstances, but that's only on the surface, and I lay my life,' he says, 'that she's the true golden gold at heart.'

* Besides Old Harmon and Rumty, there are three other fathers whose relationship to their children is shown in *Our Mutual Friend*. These are Rogue Riderhood, who throws things at his daughter and abuses her when, supporting him after his near-drowning, she staggers under his weight; Gaffer Hexam, who tries to keep his child-ren illiterate; and Jenny Wren's father (whom she always refers to as her 'bad child') who betrays his daughter's secret for the money to drink himself to death.

The Boffins' influence has already improved Bella; now Boffin hatches an absurd but lively plot to reform her. He pretends to grow hard and mercenary, ostentatiously reading up on the lives of squalid misers (such as 'Vulture' Hopkins and the Dancers, brother and sister, who found a dead sheep when they were out walking and made it into mutton pies). Finally he denounces Rokesmith for presuming to aspire to Bella and praises her for having the sense to hold out for a rich husband. His strategy works; Bella turns on Boffin, berates herself, champions Rokesmith, and almost immediately marries him.

When we first meet her, Bella is selfish, greedy, discontented and unproductive; all these traits are expressed primarily through her relation to money. In the course of the novel she develops unstinted love, absolute trust, perfect contentment with what she has and diligence to make it suffice. She becomes a perfect wife, not only defeating Old Harmon's malicious intentions, but working them to an opposite result. The task of accomplishing this transformation convincingly is of central importance to the effect of Dickens's fable; it is a difficult challenge, and one met with less than total success. Dickens shows adequately Bella's potentialities for change and the pressures which change her; he makes convincing the necessary direction and the logical implications of her change. But in driving home the logic of her reform he makes her less attractive than he means her to be. He insists too rigidly on the completeness of her conversion, and when she is converted, he seems to have no resources except an occasionally unfortunate arch-ness of tone with which to keep up her sprightliness.

Dickens starts out well with Bella. Her pettishness and self-absorption amidst the constant back-biting and shifting alliances of her lower middle class home are convincing; the mixture of her irritation with her mother's pretence of status and her involvement in this pretence is well-calculated. Dickens lets her talk vigor-ously and, given her premises, sensibly:

'It was ridiculous enough to know I shouldn't like him – how *could* I like him, left to him in a will, like a dozen of spoons, with everything cut and dried beforehand, like orange chips! Talk of orange flowers indeed! I declare again it's shame! Those ridiculous points would have been smoothed away by the money, for I love money, and want money – want it dreadfully. I hate to be poor, and we are degradingly poor, offensively poor, miserably poor, beastly poor.' (Bk. 1, Chap. 4)

The change that begins to come over her as she stays with the Boffins is thought out and presented with sophistication and authority. It is shown in the form of an increased self-consciousness which seems on the verge of applying standards to the motives which it recognizes. Bella, as she declares that she is mercenary, that she cares extraordinarily for what money will buy, that she has come to the conclusion that she absolutely must marry for money, begins to judge herself. She is conscious of cutting a poor figure before Boffin's secretary; she knows he is aware she hasn't communicated with her family since she left them. Partly to show herself that she is not utterly selfish, partly to show Rokesmith, she spends a present from Boffin on her father – she buys him a suit and takes him to lunch – and she begins to show her father's redeeming but hitherto severely muffled influence. Bella meets Lizzie Hexam, the daughter of the man who recovered John Harmon's supposed corpse from the Thames. Lizzie takes her into her confidence, which flatters and touches Bella; she is struck by the contrast Lizzie's selflessness and calm dedication to a hopeless love makes with her own self-avowed greed and triviality, and she is moved by Lizzie's assumption that they both have the same standards.

All this is adequate to the challenge of Dickens's undertaking. But when Bella has made her decisive choice and married Rokesmith, she becomes less convincing and less interesting. Both her husband and Dickens are concerned with Bella's being free from all taint of concern for money, and the completeness of her cure is wearisomely pounded home, until she seems more fixed on money than ever before. She is made to say over and over how content she is with their hundred and fifty pounds a year: 'We have all we want and more'; 'Dear John, it's not possible you think we are poor?'; 'I don't want a carriage, believe me'; 'I want nothing on earth, and I want you to believe it'; 'I believe, dear John, that you believe that I believe that we have as much money as we require' (Bk. IV, Chap. 5). It is not only this excessive emphasis that makes her disappointing as a reformed character. Dickens's tone with her grows arch – oppressively so when she is with her father; he makes her more and more of a Ruth Pinch, a winning little woman with winning little ways. He plunges her into her housekeeping in her 'charmingest of doll's houses'

(Bk. iv, Chap. 5) on Blackheath. He rubs his hands over her pretty little domestic endeavours:

Such weighing and mixing and chopping and grating, such dusting and washing and polishing, such snipping and weeding and trowelling and other small gardening, such making and mending and folding and airing, such diverse arrangements, and above all such severe study! For Mrs J. H., who had never been wont to do too much at home as Miss B. W., was under the constant necessity of referring for advice and support to a sage volume entitled The Complete British Family Housewife, which she would sit consulting, with her elbows on the table, and her temples on her hands, like some perplexed enchantress poring over the Black Art. (Bk. iv, Chap. 5)

This is the woman who gave Ibsen his famous phrase. Bella says: 'I want to be something so much worthier than the doll in the doll's house' (Bk. iv, Chap. 5). Her idea of worthiness (an idea which Dickens evidently shares) seems to be the ability to have absolute faith in her husband: 'Try me through some reverse, John – try me through some trial – and tell them after *that* what you think of me' (Bk. iv, Chap. 5). John promises to do so; he already has a trial in mind. He knows the police are looking for Julius Handford (one of his aliases) and that he will eventually be found and held on suspicion of involvement in his own murder. He has postponed clearing up this problem, because he wants to give Bella her occasion: ' "She shall see me under suspicion of having murdered myself, and *you* shall see how trusting and how true she'll be" ' (Bk. iv, Chap. 13). In the event, Bella's first reaction to the information that her husband is suspected of 'the murder of John Harmon, your allotted husband' is 'a burst of generous indignation. "My beloved husband, how dare they!" ' Her second is a declaration of absolute trust:

'If I could not trust you, I should fall dead at your feet.'

The kindling triumph in his face was bright, indeed, as he looked up and rapturously exclaimed, what had he done to deserve the blessing of this dear, confiding creature's heart! Again she put her hand upon his lips, saying, 'Hush!' and then told him, in her own little natural, pathetic way, that if all the world were against him she would be for him; that if all the world repudiated him, she would believe him; that if he were infamous in other eyes, he would be honoured in hers; and that, under the worst unmerited suspicion, she could devote her life to consoling him, and imparting her own faith in him to their little child. (Bk. IV, Chap. 12)

It seems not too far-fetched to suspect that some of the emphasis in this statement of faith derives from Dickens's own position when he wrote it – knowing that the facts of his relationship with Ellen Ternan made him a guilty man, wanting to be justified, understood, exculpated. But Dickens evidently thinks of Bella's rapturous immersion in her mate as womanhood's crowning glory, the moral goal towards which Bella has been struggling. However inadequate the figure evoked by his rhetoric may seem to us as a vision of human excellence, however much this fervour of confidence may seem a response to Dickens's private emotional needs, as opposed to the needs of his drama, we should admit the logic of his asserting the qualities of complete trust and immersion in another person as the opposites of the selfishness and separateness of the mercenary person.

The subplot of *Our Mutual Friend*, which concerns the love between Lizzie Hexam and Eugene Wrayburn, is a close parallel to the main story. Both plots show the development of an unselfish love against the opposition of false values in the lovers' backgrounds. In both, the moral drama concentrates on one of the lovers, whose potentialities for good are to be brought out by the other. Eugene is parallel to Bella – badly in need of redemption, conscious that he ought to be better than he is, self-willed (although, in his case, the will lies behind a formula of apathy and purposelessness). He follows in the James Harthouse – Henry Gowan tradition of aristocratic negligence, but is much more sympathetic than either of them. Dickens shows that Eugene really is unhappy in his situation, and that, like Bella's, his standards and impulses are fundamentally decent and delicate.

The two couples have parallel relations to the generation before; the values of Bella's mother and of Eugene's father are resented and ridiculed by the children these values have corrupted, and while Gaffer Hexam has much better intentions than Old Harmon had, he stands in much the same relation to his child's development. Gaffer's business is robbing the bodies in the Thames – both he and Old Harmon get their living from London's sordid refuse. He is fiercely anxious to keep his children from learning to read and write. Thus both John and Lizzie must defeat their fathers' intentions and rise above the origins symbolized by their fathers' occupations. But their origins are, nevertheless, in various ways vital to the success of their loves: In Lizzie's case this point is made with especial vividness.

Wrayburn's father is not seen in the novel, but his

bad influence is insisted upon. This influence is to be understood as something claimed by Wrayburn rather than something proved; Wrayburn always blames his own shortcomings on circumstances beyond his control. His characteristic manner and attitude of being in a position he despises (assisting at one of the Veneerings' dinner parties or drifting toward an attempt to seduce Lizzie) but being helpless to do anything about it, is appropriate to his situation in life – he is a barrister and, as he says, 'I hate my profession'. His father set his destiny; he had no choice:

'M.R.F. [my respected father] having always in the clearest manner provided [as he calls it] for his children by prearranging from the hour of the birth of each, and sometimes from an earlier period, what the devoted little victim's calling and course in life should be, M. R. F. prearranged for myself that I was to be the barrister I am [with the slight addition of an enormous practice, which has not accrued] and also the married man I am not.' (Bk. 1, Chap. 12)

Dickens takes pains to drive home the implications with respect to love and marriage of Mr Wrayburn's attitude towards his sons:

'My respected father has found, down in the parental neighbourhood, a wife for his not-generally-respected son.'
'With some money, of course?'
'With some money, of course, or he would not have found her.' (Bk. 1, Chap. 12)

Musing on his relation to Lizzie just before Headstone batters him into the river, Wrayburn for the first time seems to consider marrying the girl. But he immediately invokes his father to suppress the idea. His father, he knows, would remind him of his character, his principles and his situation: 'You wouldn't marry for some money and some station because you were frightfully likely to become bored. Are you less frightfully likely to become bored, marrying for no money and no station? Are you sure of yourself!' Eugene decides that he would have to admit: 'Good reasoning on part of M. R. F. *Not* sure of myself' (Bk. iv, Chap. 6).

But when Eugene has married Lizzie and his father has seen her, all goes well. Mr Wrayburn, a connoisseur of beauty, asserts that Lizzie's portrait ought to be painted; he tastes the claret he has been served and says, ' "My dear son, why do you drink this trash?" ' – a question 'tantamount in him' – Eugene later says, 'to a paternal benediction on our union, accompanied by a gush of tears' (Bk. iv, Chap. 16). This outcome is consistent with the class assessments of *Our Mutual Friend*, which ferociously attacks new money and the upper bourgeoisie but allows decency and honour to the representatives of the old gentry – Eugene, Mortimer Lightwood, the Rev. Milvey, Twemlow. Although capable of arranging advantageous marriages for his children, Mr Wrayburn can accept with grace the *fait accompli* of his son's marriage to Lizzie, and furthermore is able to understand his son's action and to appreciate Lizzie's true excellence when he sees it.

Lizzie, whose origins could hardly be lower, is perhaps the most attractive young woman in Dickens. Dickens often sets out to create examples of female perfection – Agnes Wickfield, Esther Summerson and

Amy Dorrit, for instance. All of his previous attempts have been more severely conditioned than Lizzie is by a specific concept of the feminine role. Lizzie is not a little Dickens woman, bustling about unobtrusively with a basket of keys; we do not see her domestic virtues, but her courage, her resolve, her independence, her presence of mind, her steady skill in an emergency. Previous heroines have these traits too, but always more specifically in a woman's sphere. With Lizzie they are human qualities, not feminine qualities. A parallel difference lies in Dickens's altered moral requirements. Agnes, Esther, and Amy, as ideal women, are required to be not only unselfish but self-sacrificing to a degree which would be considered monstrous in a man. It is possible that Agnes would have married Uriah Heep to save her father, and Esther plans to marry Jarndyce out of duty. Such heroines are not allowed to remind others that they are persons too, with rights and lives. Lizzie does not hesitate to do so:

'It grieves you to see me distressed, Mr Wrayburn, it grieves me to see you distressed. I don't reproach you. Indeed I don't reproach you. You have not felt this as I feel it, being so different from me, and beginning from another point of view. You have not thought. But I entreat you to think now, think now!'

'What am I to think of?' asked Eugene bitterly.

'Think of me.' (Bk. IV, Chap. 6)

Lizzie is asking Eugene to consider the consequence to herself of an affair between them – a safe enough subject for a feminine plea for consideration (although startling and appealing in its implicit admission that Lizzie, for all her strength, has a heart and body subject to being seduced). But she is just as resolute when her brother asks her to give her up her plan to let Eugene educate her, and when he wants her to marry Headstone, become 'respectable', and thus advance his prospects. It never enters her head to sacrifice herself for her brother, and she clearly has no regrets for her inability to do so, but only shame for her brother's selfishness.

Lizzie's unselfishness, closely involved with her love but lacking any suggestion of an extreme and arbitrary sexual attribute, becomes felt as a life-giving principle to set against the deadly boredom of Eugene's way of life and of the 'Society' with which he helplessly drifts. Eugene's moral rescue, like Bella's, takes place through the development in him of a reciprocal unselfish love. Lizzie understands what he needs; as she tells Jenny Wren, his failings have 'grown up through his being like one cast away, for the want of something to trust in, and care for, and think well of'. But she has no hope of filling herself what she calls the 'empty place' in Eugene. As she tells Bella, 'I have no more dreamed of being his wife than he has, and words could not be stronger than that' (Bk. III, Chap. 9). The only thing she can do when it becomes clear that Eugene is pursuing her is to hide, to find work outside London.

Faced with the problem of bringing Eugene and Lizzie together without violating the character he has given Eugene, Dickens resorts to melodrama, which he handles with great skill and appropriate symbolism. Bradley Headstone clubs Eugene and pushes him into the Thames; Lizzie rescues him; he marries her on what seems to be his death-bed, rallies and recovers – this is the bare outline of Dickens's melodrama, and perhaps sounds foolish and arbitrary. It is not. To see why not we have to look first at Headstone, a figure without a parallel in the other plot (although we can see in him a similar function to the fierce malice expressed in Old Harmon's will; he is a deadly danger to the lovers, but becomes against his intentions a bridge between them). Headstone is not an arbitrary convenience but a carefully worked out emblematic figure. He has offered honourable marriage to Lizzie and been refused; he has tried to warn Eugene, as a seducer, away from her, and Eugene has treated him with cool contempt. In conventional terms Headstone is completely in the right, and in terms of the Carlylean values of work and earnestness which Dickens usually asserts he is incomparably the better man. His heart is in his work; it is good work; he does it as well as he can, sparing no pains, while Eugene lounges and smokes. Are we then to prefer Eugene simply because he is graceful and clever and a gentleman, able to make the dogged and mechanical Headstone look foolish? But in making Headstone the villain and Eugene the hero, Dickens is not abandoning but discriminating among his usual moral insistences. Headstone is actually a morally repellent figure, and a close examination shows why; he is immensely selfish. His selfishness, which dwarfs that of any other character in the book, takes the two forms of ambition and passion, and is vividly reflected in his matrimonial project.

Headstone's ambition is the direct occasion of his first meeting Lizzie. An ex-pauper lad, anxious to suppress his origins, he greatly prizes respectability; he has been urging Lizzie's brother to drop his illiterate and dubiously respectable sister: 'You see, Hexam, you will be one of us' (Bk. II, Chap. I). Urged by Charley to see the girl and verify that she is not disreputable, he immediately falls in love and begins to consider making her worthy of him:

'Some man who had worked his way might come to admire – your sister – and might even in time bring himself to think of marrying – your sister – and it would be a sad drawback and a heavy penalty upon him, if, overcoming in his mind other inequalities of condition and other considerations against it, this inequality and this consideration [Lizzie's illiteracy] remained in full force.' (Bk. II, Chap. I)

Headstone's passion is, if anything, more selfish than his ambition. Here he is, making his proposal of marriage:

'Yes! you are the ruin – the ruin – the ruin – of me. I have no resource in myself, I have no confidence in myself, I have no government of myself, when you are near me or in my thoughts. And you are always in my thoughts now. I have never been quit of you since I first saw you. Oh, that was a wretched day for me! That was a wretched, miserable day!' (Bk. II, Chap. 15)

He tries to show the advantages of yielding to this passion:

'My circumstances are quite easy, and you would want for nothing. My reputation stands quite high, and would be a shield for yours. If you saw me at my work, able to do it well and respected in it, you might even come to take a sort of pride in me; – I would try hard that you should. Whatever considerations I may have thought of against this offer, I have conquered, and I make it with all my heart.' (Bk. II, Chap. 15)

Headstone goes on to mention that the marriage would help Lizzie's brother. Charley reinforces his plea: 'As Mr Headstone's wife you would be occupying a most respectable station, and you would be holding a far better place in society than you hold now. . . .' (Bk. ii, Chap. 15). Charley not only hopes to profit from Headstone's influence in his profession; he has developed Headstone's anxiety about being tainted, an anxiety especially strong now that his sister seems potentially a gentleman's prey.

If Lizzie were to accept Headstone, her motives would presumably be an amalgam of Lady Dedlock's in marrying Sir Leicester and Louisa Gradgrind's in marrying Bounderby. Headstone's motive is a totally selfish passion; Dickens makes even more strongly the point he made in *Great Expectations* – that passion is no proof of unselfishness in love, although it may be 'disinterested' in the sense of being at odds with a man's rational interest.

Headstone's reaction to Lizzie's rejection of his proposal is to determine to murder the man she loves. He must do this in a passion, righteously enraged by the sight of the two together. And it seems that he cannot strike until Eugene has overcome his indecisions and made his guilty resolution.

As the ripple under the moon broke unexpectedly now and then, and palely flashed in a new shape and with a new sound, so parts of his thoughts started, unbidden, from the rest, and revealed their wickedness. 'Out of the question to marry her,' said Eugene, 'and out of the question to leave her. The crisis!'

He had sauntered far enough. Before turning to retrace his

172

steps, he stopped upon the margin, to look down at the reflected night. In an instant, with a dreadful crash, the reflected night turned crooked, flames shot jaggedly through the air, and the moon and stars came bursting from the sky. (Bk. IV, Chap. 6)

Headstone has struck; this is the beginning of perhaps the most strikingly effective description of violence in all of Dickens. Lizzie, walking nearby, hears the 'sound of blows' falling 'heavily and cruelly on the quiet of the night'; she hears 'a faint groan' and a splash: 'Her old bold life and habit instantly inspired her' (Bk. IV, Chap. 6). Dickens describes the rescue in careful detail, making the point that Lizzie is probably the only woman in England who could have done it. Not only her courage and presence of mind, but all her old skills are demanded, she gauges the speed of the current, guesses correctly where Eugene will bob up again if he does, sees the slight ripple he makes, waits to seize his hair until she can get it securely and not push him under, knows how to hitch him and tow him. The point is clear. Lizzie's origins, specifically the horrible trade she has helped her father ply, enable her to save her lover. Her fidelity towards her past, her refusal of her brother's repeated demands that she deny it and become respectable, acquire a new perspective. At the moment of crisis Lizzie's history of always doing what she can in the place where she finds herself enables her to accomplish the, to her, ultimately important task, which would otherwise be impossible.

Dickens's way of making this point is, for all its graphic crudity, effective and moving. In a society in which a large section of the population – including Dickens himself – was anxious to suppress knowledge of their parents' or grandparents' occupations, removing themselves earnestly from their origins and grasping for the respectability so desperately sought by Headstone and Charley Hexam, it is fine to see the proposition so firmly established that what is a social shame may be a human strength, that what we are, what we know, what we can do is more important than our social respectability.

Eugene, like John Harmon, acquires from his near-drowning a saving distance from his previous life and previous identity, a perspective which makes him desperately anxious to marry Lizzie before he dies. His impulse to marry turns out to have been an instinct for life; married, he gains new determination and mends quickly. Thus Lizzie saves him again; her qualities as a person are in every way, literally and emblematically, necessary to his life.

The marriage between Lizzie and Eugene is the last one made in Dickens's novels. In several ways it is worthy of its position. It is, of course, unmercenary – Lizzie has nothing and Eugene is in debt. There is a strong probability (in no way regarded) that Eugene's people will cut him off for marrying Lizzie. The marriage is made for love, but not for physical passion; Eugene is at the point of death when he marries, battered and broken. The marriage is desperately needed by both parties; Eugene's need is especially clear and pressing, but Lizzie has previously determined to cherish by herself her love for Eugene and has admitted that her life may prove to be 'but a weary one' (Bk. III, Chap. 9). Although Lizzie comes from the lowest level of society and Eugene from almost the highest, there is as little as possible sense that he is raising her, bettering her position. We are made to see both Eugene and Lizzie as human beings, rather than as occupants of class positions.

Dickens ends the novel by subjecting this marriage to the judgment of the group which meets around the Veneerings' dinner table. Lady Tippins plays 'Chairwoman of Committees' and sets herself to 'what-you-may-call-it – elicit, I suppose – the voice of Society'. She states the question:

'The question before the committee is whether a young man of very fair family, good appearance and some talent, makes a fool or a wise man of himself in marrying a female waterman, turned factory girl.'

Mortimer Lightwood resists the description of Lizzie in these terms, and when Podsnap demands 'was this young woman ever a female waterman?' and 'was she ever . . . a factory girl?' he denies both facts, but admits that 'she rowed in a boat with her father', and 'she had some employment in a paper mill'. This is taken by the company as mere quibbling and evasion. Of course, it is not. Lightwood is refusing to accept the validity, in such an important human concern as that of marriage, of classifying people by their backgrounds and occupations. To Lady Tippins and Podsnap, as to Headstone and Charley Hexam, class background, money and social position are all important. Charley Hexam's drive for 'respectability', Podsnap's use of 'respectability' to crush opposition, and the oddly complete lack of origins of the Veneerings are all aspects of the same thing – a barren, selfish system of values which sees no goals but those of grasping and wielding power, and which is particularly horrible and inhuman when it applies itself to marrying and giving in marriage.

Twemlow is, besides Lightwood, the only member of the company who does not accept this system of values. He maintains that 'if the gentleman's feelings of respect, of admiration, and affection induced him to marry this lady, . . . he is the greater gentleman for the action . . .'. Twemlow defines 'gentleman': 'I beg to say that, when I use the word gentleman, I use it in the sense in which the degree may be attained by any man'. This is not a cheapening of the word. Twemlow's, and Dickens's, kind of gentility is a moral category, and cannot be bought. It is, no doubt, unreasonably optimistic to imply that any man may attain it, but we may be glad that Dickens did not lose his sense of the potentialities of human nature for moral excellence, nor his hatred of those points of view which construct their elites on more exclusive criteria than those of love, gratitude, and decency.